C000133157

Teaching Dyslexics How to Read and Write Music

DEBORAH ALOBA

First published by Shakspeare Editorial, October 2020

ISBNs pbk 978-1-9993295-0-1
        ebk 978-1-9993295-1-8

Copyright © 2020 Deborah Aloba

deborahaloba.com

No part of this publication may be reproduced, stored in a
retrieval system, or transmitted, in any form or by any means
mechanical, electronic, photocopying, recording or otherwise
without the prior written consent of the publisher; nor be
otherwise circulated in any form of binding or cover other than
that in which it is published and without a similar condition
being imposed on the subsequent purchaser.

The right of Deborah Aloba to be identified as the author of
the work has been asserted by her in accordance with the
Copyright, Designs and Patents Act 1988.

Illustrations © Deborah Aloba and Christine Wong (except for
p. 166 –123rf.com; p. 171 – Pixabay and creative commons)

Design and typesetting www.ShakspeareEditorial.org

I dedicate this book to my grandparents
Reginald and Muriel Crozier

And to my mother
Yvonne Aloba

Who have supported and encouraged me throughout my life

CONTENTS

ILLUSTRATIONS

13. Causes of Dyslexia

FOREWORD

Your passion and determination to find ways of reaching dyslexic people is inspiring and I hope that more music teachers adopt the invaluable techniques you have uncovered so that everyone can enjoy learning music.

C. Napper (student's mother)

I have Sjögren's syndrome and this causes me to suffer with visual stress, in the course of reading this book, I have realised that if I read on blue coloured paper this enables me to read with more clarity and my concentration levels are greatly enhanced.

Sally Clarke

I have a scientific background and very early on working with Deborah we established that what I feel when I sing is different from what people normally experience – and is often completely backwards. Through her work in adapting her teaching to me and allowing me to process her instruction in my own way, my voice has grown and developed in ways I would never have thought possible. I don't think I would have made the same progress had I been forced into working with what I **should** *have been feeling or without the visual imagery to help.*

Emma Walker

1. INTRODUCTION

Several years ago, a young student came to my music studio for her first lesson. She was nervous, but I wasn't particularly concerned, as I know I have a skill for putting my students at ease. I knew she had dyslexia, but as this was our first lesson together I did not consider this to be a particular problem.

As the lesson commenced, I could see her anxiety levels rising. I reassured her again and again, speaking gently, that we would just take it slowly, that there was no rush, no pressure. She was not reassured.

Her mother, who was with her, attempted to reassure her, it did not help.

She had a beautiful soprano voice, but nothing I said stemmed her anxiety. When she left my studio, she left in a state of anxiety. I was determined that no other student would ever have that experience with me again and so began my research into the impact that dyslexia has on musicians. I resolved to find a way of teaching that gave them the same opportunities as non-dyslexic musicians.

As I began to read academic papers, search the internet and look for books that would give me the information I needed about what aids and methods were available for teaching the dyslexic musician, two things became obvious:

1. Much of the information on the benefits of aids and methods was based on anecdotal evidence
2. There was no one place that I could go to get the information I needed to assist my students.

So I decided to test the anecdotal evidence to see if the aids and methods referred to in the research literature actually worked. The information in this book is based on the results of those tests and the application of the aids and methods I have found to be most effective when teaching my dyslexic students.

The reason I have written this book is because I do not want any other music teacher, parent, or indeed any adult dyslexic student, to have to spend the many hours that I have spent, searching for effective aids and methods for teaching how to read and write music.

Furthermore, I do not want young musicians with dyslexia or any other learning difficulty to give up on pursuing a career in music using the traditional route. Having studied in both the UK and the USA, I can confirm that the traditional route of conservatoires and universities requires students to have achieved at least a Grade 8 in their music exams. Even if a student is extremely talented and attains a place at their chosen conservatoire or university, without these grades, there is normally a proviso attached. What is the proviso? That they must get to grips with music theory in their first year.

The great news is that once they are at university in the UK, they will get a superb level of support. However, it is the years in between that can be difficult, as there is limited support, which largely depends on the school's and the individual's parent's/guardian's resources. If dyslexic musicians do not obtain effective teaching in their formative years, many drop out of music or give up on their dream of music as a career. I don't believe you should ever give up on your dreams.

During my journey to discover effective aids and methods to teach my dyslexic students I have observed the following:

(a) Many music teachers, parents and adults have a very limited understanding of the causes of dyslexia.

(b) There is limited knowledge of how dyslexia manifests itself or the impact it can have on a student's ability to read and write music and take music exams.

(c) The causes and reasons for dyslexia have been researched for over 100 years and, although the purpose of this book is to provide an insight into aids and methods that can be applied when teaching a dyslexic student, I thought you might be interested in the 'Why'. So I have included a chapter at the end which gives a brief insight into the three main theories on why someone is dyslexic.

(d) I have also been surprised that so few teachers and parents use assistive technology to help their dyslexic students. Although the benefits of assistive technology have been studied for the last 30 years, it is only recently that iPads, tablets, laptops, computers, apps and so on have been used in education to assist dyslexics with their reading and writing. The thought occurred to me some time ago that assistive technology incorporated many of the multi-sensory elements that were necessary for the effective teaching of dyslexic music students. As a result of this light-bulb moment I began to use Musescore, a free notation software program to prepare revision exercises and revision papers for my students. Without exception they love it. I had to explain that they would still need to take their exams on paper. However, just knowing that they could get great results by using this method has given them confidence. It has also provided me with a greater insight into what they require when they do work on paper.

It is a constant joy to see my students' progress, pass exams, become excited about composition and gain confidence in their musical abilities. Yes, it can take longer sometimes to see results, but I have learnt so many new teaching skills on our journeys together, and I have gained a wonderful insight into how to look at music and life from a different perspective.

Let us start at the beginning. Exactly what is dyslexia and how can it manifest itself when your student is trying to learn how to read and write music?

The British Dyslexia Association (BDA) adopted Sir J. Rose's definition of dyslexia in 2009:

Dyslexia is a learning difficulty that primarily affects the skills involved in accurate and fluent word reading and spelling. Characteristic features of dyslexia are difficulties in phonological awareness, verbal memory and verbal processing speed. Dyslexia occurs across the range of intellectual abilities. It is best thought of as a continuum, not a distinct category, and there are no clear cut-off points. Co-occurring difficulties may be seen in aspects of language, motor co-ordination, mental calculation, concentration and personal organisation, but these are not, by themselves, markers of dyslexia. A good indication of the severity and persistence of dyslexic difficulties can be gained by examining how the individual responds or has responded to well-founded intervention.

In addition to these characteristics:

The BDA acknowledges the visual and auditory processing difficulties that some individuals with dyslexia can experience. It points out that dyslexic readers can show a combination of abilities and difficulties that affect the learning process. The BDA acknowledge that many dyslexics have strengths in other areas, such as design, problem solving, creative skills, interactive skills and oral skills.

And, just to prove them right, some famous dyslexics are Albert Einstein, Mohammed Ali, Cher, Tony Bennett and Robbie Williams.

It is accepted that many people who suffer with dyslexia encounter visual problems that can present themselves as:

- headaches and eyestrain when reading
- text blurring
- text going in and out of focus

- text appearing double
- text alternating between single and double
- difficulty keeping place in text
- difficulty tracking across lines of text
- difficulty because of brightness of the page
- difficulty because of contrast between text and background
- text appearing to shimmer or flicker.

Dyslexics can find it difficult to read for any length of time because it is exhausting. If your student has difficulty reading one line of written text, can you imagine the frustration and confusion when they are faced with a music score that has seven components within it.

These components include music notes, symbols, numbers, English and foreign languages, lyrics and dynamic markings, which are printed in, on or near a music stave, and they all need to be visually processed and deciphered. Just take a moment to imagine a section of music, now imagine all those components blurring or floating across the page or merging into each other. I hope that you can now begin to understand the level of visual stress a dyslexic music student might experience. I am sure you will now appreciate that they can be overwhelmed by the complexity of the information that needs to be unravelled just to start the process of learning a piece of music or a song.

Some students may not only be dyslexic but may also have challenges when writing and be dysgraphic. The difficulties they could face are:

- forming letters/music notes
- spacing notes correctly on the stave
- writing music on the correct line of a stave
- making letters and music notes the correct size
- holding paper with one hand while writing with the other
- holding and controlling writing tools
- putting the right amount of pressure on the paper with a writing tool
- maintaining the right arm position and posture for writing music
- remembering to colour in the note heads
- remembering to add stems to the note heads
- remembering to write the music notes the right way round.

As one of my student's once said to me, 'It is really hard to do writing because my eye gets tired and my hands get tired, it strains my brain really.'

CHECKLIST

1. What is the definition of dyslexia?
2. Name 6 ways in which visual stress in dyslexia may manifest itself.
3. Name 6 challenges that a dyslexic may face when writing music.

It is accepted that the best method of teaching dyslexics to read or write text or music is to use a multi-sensory approach. There is no one method that you will be able apply when teaching a dyslexic student. You will need to experiment by using the different methods in this book to see what combination of aids works best for each student.

How a dyslexic absorbs information can have a significant impact on their ability to learn a new skill. To become a musician, a student needs techniques and skills to sing or to play an instrument and to read and write music. In the course of absorbing the information required to learn a new skill, it has been established that everyone has a preference in how they learn, be it visually, aurally or kinaesthetically. A 1997 study by Rose and Nicholl showed that dyslexic students could have a dominant preference when learning, which broke down as:

- 25%–30% visual
- 25%–30% auditory
- 15% kinaesthetic

- while 25%–30% preferred mixed modalities.

A further study undertaken by Exley in 2003 discovered that 5 out 7 dyslexic children aged 7–8 years preferred a kinaesthetic approach when learning. In 2007, while evaluating adults with learning difficulties, Lisle discovered that:

- 34% of participants were visual learners
- 34% were auditory learners
- 23% kinaesthetic learners
- 6% used a combination of visual, auditory and kinaesthetic learning (multimodal).

A 2010 study by Stampoltzis et al. also supported results that a kinaesthetic learning style was preferred by dyslexic participants. These findings were reinforced by Andreou and Vlachos in 2013, when they assessed learning styles in typical readers and dyslexic adolescents and noted that many adolescents with dyslexia were 'kinaesthetic, auditory kinaesthetic and then visual-auditory'. These results show that dyslexic adolescents predominantly use a multimodal approach when learning.

During the first few lessons with a student I note how they absorb information and consider whether they respond better when I give them:

a) a visual instruction

> *Imagine the breath you are inhaling is a colour. It journeys through your mouth, down your trachea, into your lungs, making them expand, which in turn makes the ribcage that encases your lungs expand …*

b) a kinaesthetic instruction

> *Place your hand on your lower abdomen, between your belly button and your pelvic floor, now take a breath. Can you feel the expansion in your body? …*

c) an aural instruction

> *Listen to your breath as you inhale. Does it sound shallow and sharp, or deep and full?*

d) or do they respond best to a mixture of all three?

e) I also note whether there are any problems with their ability to hear/listen.

My students are introduced to videos of MRI scans of how the vocal tract, lungs, diaphragm and abdomen function during the singing process, this engages them both visually and aurally. I also introduce them to pictures and photos of the vocal tract, lungs and so on, so that they gain a clear understanding of their vocal instrument.

I find the following YouTube videos invaluable when teaching:

videos of vocal chords/larynx

https://www.youtube.com/watch?v=-1Fv7IPmJo4, https://www.youtube.com/watch?v=iYpDwhpILkQ

https://www.youtube.com/watch?v=-XGds2GAvGQ&t=118s

MRI scans of singers singing

https://www.youtube.com/watch?v=YIUvX7hebBA, https://www.youtube.com/watch?v=f5SUhhfwxEl

https://www.youtube.com/watch?v=M2OdAp7MJAI&t=153s

CHECKLIST

1. What has been established as the best method of teaching a dyslexic music student?
2. How can you assess whether your dyslexic music student prefers visual, auditory or kinaesthetic learning?
3. Have you noted any hearing or listening issues?

4. ASSESSING IF A STUDENT HAS A LEARNING DIFFICULTY

In 2019 the All Party Parliamentary Group for Dyslexia (ApPGD) published their examination of the support for dyslexics in education and found that it was in a very poor state. They acknowledged that diagnosis was poor, unless parents could afford a private assessment. The ApPGD report confirmed that over 80% of pupils were still leaving school without having been properly assessed and diagnosed. It accepted that support was either inadequate or non-existent.

Although parents are aware that their child may be dyslexic, in many instances they do not have a formal diagnosis because they simply cannot afford it. Assessments cost between £400 and £700. It is interesting to note that dyslexia can be a hereditary condition.

Many children who are dyslexic are incredible lateral thinkers and find ways of coping that can also mask potential problems at school. Within the classroom they may present as unruly or act as the class clown, to deflect attention from the difficulties they are facing. Teachers have limited training in how to deal with dyslexic students and heavy workloads. Therefore, children who do not have a formal assessment are not always given the support they need with reading and writing, let alone with learning music other than by ear.

So how am I, as a singing/music teacher, alerted to the possibility that a new student may have dyslexia or a learning difficulty? If a parent, guardian or adult student says that a diagnosis has been made, I am starting from a solid, informed base. Even if a diagnosis has not been made a parent may still tell me of their concerns, but quite often they say nothing (especially if the child comes from certain cultural backgrounds).

If, after four or five sessions with my new student, they appear to be having problems processing my instructions, I am immediately alerted that there may be difficulties with their ability to unpack the information I am conveying.

You could say, 'Well, you might not be imparting the information clearly.' Although that is a possibility, I have been teaching for 25 years and during that period most students have understood my instructions and made progress.

You might say, 'Well, it is very early days.'

That would also be a valid observation. However, in those 25 years I have learnt that there are certain instructions that the majority of students understand within a very short time.

When a new student is not making the progress I would expect, I make a note of the indicators that are causing me concern, such as:

- they don't want to look at the written music and would rather learn the piece by ear
- they can't seem to remember the melody or the lyrics of a piece we are working on
- they don't seem to understand the instructions I am giving them
- they appear to understand the instructions I am giving them, but they are doing something totally different when they perform the instruction
- they seem unable to concentrate for any length of time
- they hesitate when there is a rest in the music
- they avoid writing music
- they seem anxious throughout a lesson
- they get frustrated at certain points during the lesson
- there are moments when their body freezes
- they sing the lyrics but the words are incorrect, although similar to those written
- they want to talk a lot through their lessons
- when I ask them to clap a rhythm, they have difficulty clapping in the correct rhythm

- they are trying too hard.

I make a note of any of the above responses during the course of a lesson. If one, or a combination, of the above occur regularly, I begin casually asking questions in the course of our conversation to check if there might be a possibility of a learning difficulty such as dyslexia. At this early stage I do not make any reference to my concerns. I make sure that my questions are open-ended because that gives the student an opportunity to provide longer answers. This helps me to elicit more information for a better overview of any potential learning issues.

The sorts of questions I ask are:

- Would you mind describing what this music score looks like?
- What sort of books do you like reading?
- Would you like me to give you one instruction at a time or do you mind me asking you to do two things at the same time?
- Oh, I'm tired. I need to be careful as I get my words mixed up when I'm tired. When you get tired how does it make you feel?
- I noticed that you seem a bit worried when we got to that bit of the song, can you tell me what is worrying you about it? Why?

- We need to learn the lyrics to this song, can you read the first verse to me?
- Let's clap the rhythm of the verse.
- Could you please tell me whether you prefer the music on this size paper or this size paper?
- Can I ask you just to explain to me what you think I meant by that instruction?

My student's responses to the instructions during the lesson and to the above questions offers me an insight into whether there may be a problem.

The problem doesn't necessarily have to be dyslexia. I teach a young woman who is an astrophysicist, she is also a superb sight reader and musician generally, but after some time teaching her I noticed that if I asked her to raise her soft palette she would drop it, and if I asked her to breathe into her lower abdomen she would breathe in a higher position. I had provided a clear instruction of how to raise the soft palate and take the breath, and had even shown videos of MRI scans of the process. We had also discussed the position of the soft palate when she sang an 'ah' or 'eh' vowel, and the sensation she would feel when she took the breath into the lower abdomen. But she didn't appear able to perform the instructions and that did not make sense. I asked her to describe her understanding of what I was saying, and it very quickly became clear that when I gave her an instruction, she was processing the information backwards. If I said lift the soft palate, she would lower it, if I said breathe into the lower abdomen, she would breathe further up, nearer to the chest. Once we established the way she absorbed information and I adjusted how I delivered that information we made swift progress.

If it is not clear from my conversations with the student that there is an actual problem, I gently ask the parent/guardian or the student themselves whether there are any issues with reading and writing. With my adult students I ask if they are having problems reading and/or writing music. Depending on their response, I ask what they find difficult about the process. If parents confirm there are difficulties, then this raises a red flag that the student may be dyslexic or have some other form of learning difficulty.

If a parent, guardian or the student themselves confirms a diagnosis of dyslexia, then I request a copy of the *Dyslexia Assessment Report of Diagnostic SpLDs Assessment*. In most instances, parents are happy to share this information with me, and it is invaluable. It details the impact of that particular form of dyslexia on the student's ability to read, write and process information, and whether the student has visual stress issues or difficulties with cognitive processing. This includes issues with phonological working memory, attention and concentration. There could also be observations concerning difficulties the student has with writing, movement and coordination.

You need to be aware that this information is totally confidential and ensure that it is placed somewhere safe and is not shared with any other parties. The law requires us not to breach our obligations under the General Data Protection Regulations 2018. If I store this type of information on my computer I password protect it. If it is in paper form, I keep it in a locked drawer.

I read through the assessment report carefully and note the various issues my student may have. I then discuss the contents with them, and explain that I am going to tailor the lessons so that we can address the issues referred to in the assessment. I do this whether my student is 8 or 78. If there is any reference to visual stress, I immediately begin to explore with my student the various ways in which I can improve their issues with visual stress. Why? Because solutions can be found quite quickly (see the Visual Stress section of this book). As a student begins to resolve some of their visual stress issues, they become more confident and the teacher/student rapport should strengthen. This can lead to students feeling more able to confide when they are having difficulties during lessons. This saves time, enables issues to be pinpointed quickly and solutions to be explored – even if the solution is

accepting that an issue might take considerable time to resolve.

Sometimes dyslexics are embarrassed about their inability to read and write fluently. Many dyslexics I have taught have been excellent lateral thinkers. There have been times when it has taken me several lessons to work out that the student before me has not necessarily fully understood the instructions I have given. What they have done is made a connection between what I am saying and what they are seeing/hearing, which has enabled them to provide a correct, or almost correct, response to my query or comment. Once you have ascertained that your student may have one or more forms of dyslexia, you may want to discuss your observations with them. If you think that may undermine their confidence then, in the absence of a formal assessment, why not adapt your teaching and begin to use a multi-sensory approach?

There is no **one** method of teaching that will be successful. If a student has not been given a formal assessment you will need to be very aware of their body language. If you note a lack of concentration, their body momentarily freezing in panic or confusion on their face, you need to gently ask questions about what they are experiencing and why. Their responses will help you to understand what difficulties they have. Then you can begin to explore the best methods and aids to overcome those difficulties. Throughout the process you will need to be patient and encouraging, but it will be worth it. All my dyslexic students have been hard-working, diligent and a delight to teach.

There is one golden rule when teaching a dyslexic student, and that is the need to provide clear and concise instructions. Time and time again I have found that my dyslexic students take what I say literally. For example, I was teaching a student chords and I had explained that she needed to use the 1st, 3rd and 5th notes of the scale to create the chord. I made it perfectly clear that she needed to count the first note as 1 in the chord. She was doing extremely well. As I checked her work, I noted that the 3rd note in the D major chord was incorrect. I informed her that she needed to change the second note. She looked at me puzzled and said, 'You want me to add an E?' I was equally puzzled, but remembered to rerun exactly what I had said to her in my mind and immediately realised that she had taken me literally. I meant the second note of the chord, but she had understood what I had said as the second note of the scale. She was absolutely right, the second note of the scale was E. Once I adapted my language, there was absolutely no problem.

CHECKLIST

1. Is your student making the expected progress in their lessons?
2. Have you noticed any indicators that they may be having difficulty understanding your instructions? If so, what are those indicators?
3. How can you gently explore potential difficulties?
4. Has your exploration raised any issues that may indicate a learning difficulty?
5. If so, is it appropriate to discuss those issues with the student?
6. Have you discussed with the parent/guardian if there are any issues with reading/writing/memory?
7. If you have been informed the student is dyslexic, have you asked for a copy of their assessment?
8. If you have read the contents of the assessment, have you noted the impact that dyslexia has on your student's ability to read,write and so on?
9. Which issue do you think can be addressed to provide relatively quick and positive results?
10. Have you discussed the contents of the assessment with your student and decided on a plan of action?
11. Are you monitoring the clarity of the instructions you are giving your student?

5. VISUAL STRESS

One of the first things I discovered in the research I undertook about aids and methods to assist dyslexic students was the necessity to upsize the music. I decided to test this out and, without exception, all my dyslexic students confirmed that this made a significant difference to them. In the case of one student it immediately resolved all the issues they had with reading music.

For a student who suffers with visual stress issues the first and simplest thing to do is to upsize the music. Most music is provided on A4 paper. All you need to do is upsize the music score so that it is on A3, although you may have to upsize it to A1. I have found this invaluable with my students, and for several of them upsizing the music provided a significant improvement in their ability to read the music score.

Dyslexics find it more difficult to read black words on a white background. Numerous studies have shown that if you use a coloured background, preferably a pastel colour, this can substantially improve a student's ability to read music. As I tested this out, it became clear very quickly that this was an aid that could assist some students. What was particularly fascinating was that not one of my students chose the same colour paper as their preferred music score background colour. I had to smile when one of them informed me that pink was the best colour for them, but that they didn't like the colour pink.

Why don't you test whether your student has a preference for a particular background colour for the music score to be printed on? I have provided some examples in Figures 2a–2i to start you off.

Figure 5.1 Upsizing the music

More than you know

Words by William Rose & Edward Eliscu

Music Vincent Youmans

Figure 5.2a Music score with blue background

Figure 5.2b Music score with pink background

More than you know

Words by William Rose & Edward Eliscu
Music Vincent Youmans

Figure 5.2c Music score with yellow background

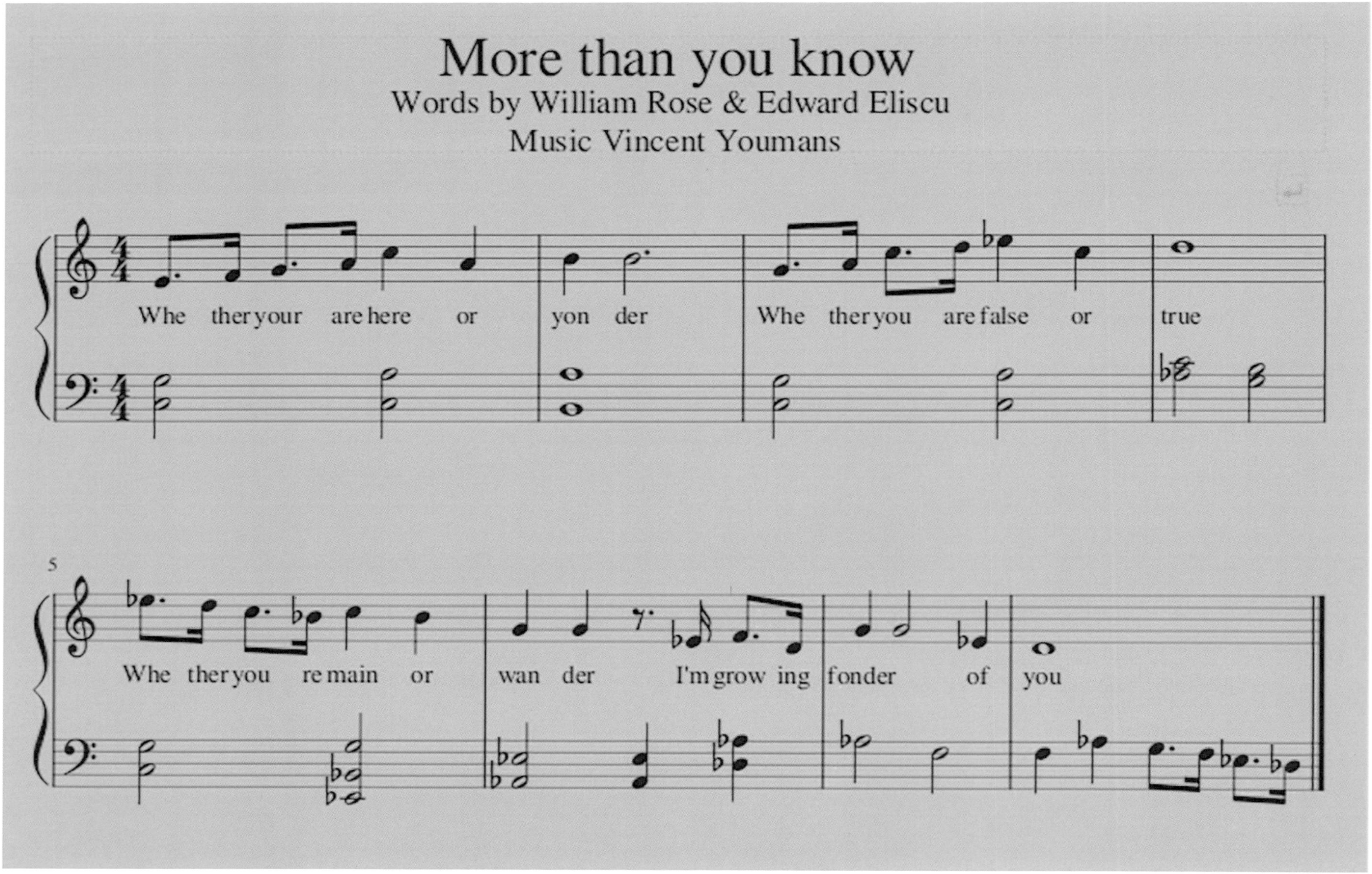

Figure 5.2d Music score with bright green background

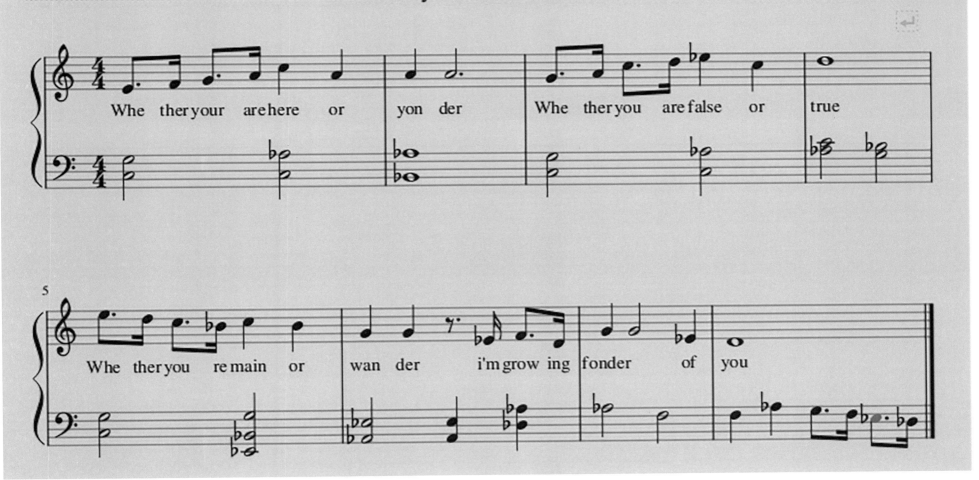

Figure 5.2e Music score with purple background

More than you know

Words by William Rose & Edward Eliscu
Music Vincent Youmans

Figure 5.2f Music score with peach background

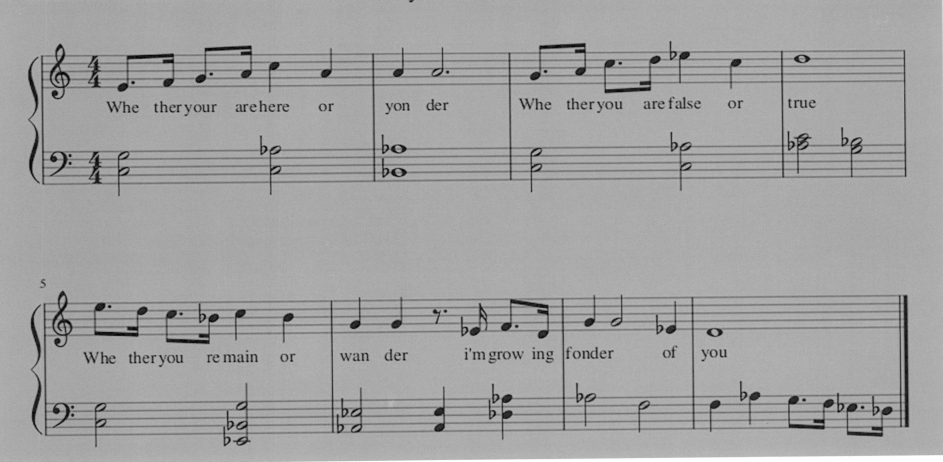

Figure 5.2g Music score with green background

More than you know

Words by William Rose & Edward Eliscu

Music Vincent Youmans

Figure 5.2h Music score with lilac background

You also might like to ask your students to experiment by going to https://www.read123.co.uk/en/glasses-tint/#gl2 There are 20 pairs of glasses on this website and all your student needs to do is click on each pair and look at the writing on the new background colour at the bottom of the page and see if one of those colours makes it easier for them to read.

Studies have shown that visual overlay sheets (VOS), which are produced in a variety of colours, can assist dyslexics to see text more clearly. Again, I tested this out. I particularly remember one student going from, 'No, no, it makes it worse,' through 'Oh, that has made it more blurry,' to 'That is a little bit better,' ending with 'Oh, I don't know how, but that makes it so much better.' It wasn't what was said that was memorable, although that was exciting enough, it was the amazement in their voice.

Figure 5.3a Pink glasses

VOS are easy to obtain, just do an internet search for 'visual overlay sheets' and a variety will appear. You do not have to buy the most expensive pack, but do buy the pack with the most pastel colours. Do make sure that you use the VOS over scores on a white background. As you try each different colour over the song/music you are working on, ask your student if they find there is any improvement in their ability to read the music. I hope you experience the sheer pleasure and joy that I feel when your student's voice changes, and you hear their wonder as they realise that they can see the music more clearly.

Figure 5.3b Green glasses

This discovery will lead to another conversation with the student or guardian. You will be surprised to discover how many dyslexics have colour-tinted glasses to assist them with their reading but, for some reason, they do not associate the necessity of using those glasses when they are reading music.

If a student doesn't already have tinted glasses, then do have a conversation with the student or their parent/guardian about having the student's eyes tested with an ophthalmologist who specialises in assessing people who suffer with visual stress.

Figure 5.3c Blue glasses

All children under the age of 16, and young adults under the age of 19 in full-time education, are entitled to a free NHS sight test with an optometrist. They are also entitled to an optical voucher to help with the cost of glasses or contact lenses. Unfortunately, the NHS sight test is only sufficiently comprehensive to enable the optometrist to assess the student's eye health and to identify the likely reasons for any visual difficulties that can affect text and music score reading. An optometrist may consider that a full assessment of binocular vision (a type of vision in which a human or animal with two eyes can perceive a single three-dimensional image of its surroundings) is necessary. This may lead to treatment by adopting eye muscle exercises. Alternatively, the optometrist may confirm that a student has visual stress issues, which may be helped by the use of visual overlay sheets or tinted lenses. Unfortunately, such an assessment or treatment programme cannot be dealt with under the NHS sight test. Your student or their parent/guardian will need to obtain this treatment privately from a specialist optometrist, or an optometrist who works in a specialist university clinic such as:

- Anglia Ruskin University
- Aston University, Birmingham
- University of Bradford
- Cardiff University
- City University of London
- Glasgow Caledonian University
- NHS Ayrshire & Arran
- Ulster University.

Some research will be required to find an appropriate specialist. If the optometrist decides that your student's visual stress can be relieved with the use of tinted glasses, then the examination and the cost of the glasses will need to be paid for privately.

Figure 5.3d Yellow glasses

It is not cheap, but the difference that it has made to some of my students has been remarkable. Not only has it increased their ability to read music scores, but it has also boosted their confidence and self-esteem. After working through the coloured overlays with one student, we saw a significant improvement when he used a darker green overlay. As a result of this discovery he went to a specialist optometrist and now has tinted glasses. It has been heart-warming to see not only how much easier it has been for him to read music but also the impact it has had on his school work. I received this lovely note from his mum, 'We wouldn't have realised X needed coloured lenses without you, so we are very grateful.'

6. USING COLOUR

There is a great deal of anecdotal evidence about the effectiveness of using colour when teaching music to dyslexic students. Again, I tested this out with my students to discover whether it was true, and found that it did assist 50% of my students. One of my students loves working with coloured notes. We even colour her nails to match the notes when we are learning to play the piano. Our only problem is that she has four fingers and one thumb – it would be helpful if she had seven fingers and a thumb!

COLOURED NOTES

I can almost hear you saying, 'But that is going to be really hard work.' Well, not when you initially start teaching music theory or an instrument. I provide my students with the note sheets shown in Figures 6.1a–1l and ask them which they prefer. Some will say black, some will say coloured and some will not mind either way, but the whole point of this exercise is to make the learning process as easy as possible.

I also find that some students find it helpful to associate a word with a note to remember what that note is called – the word must have the same sound at its beginning as the note name (see Figures 6.1e, 1f, 1i and 1l).

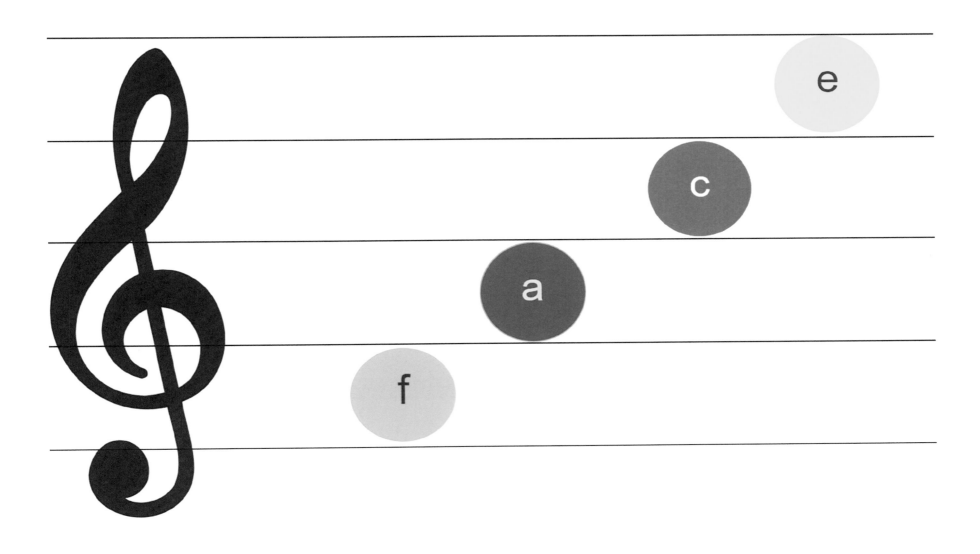

Figure 6.1a Treble clef with coloured notes

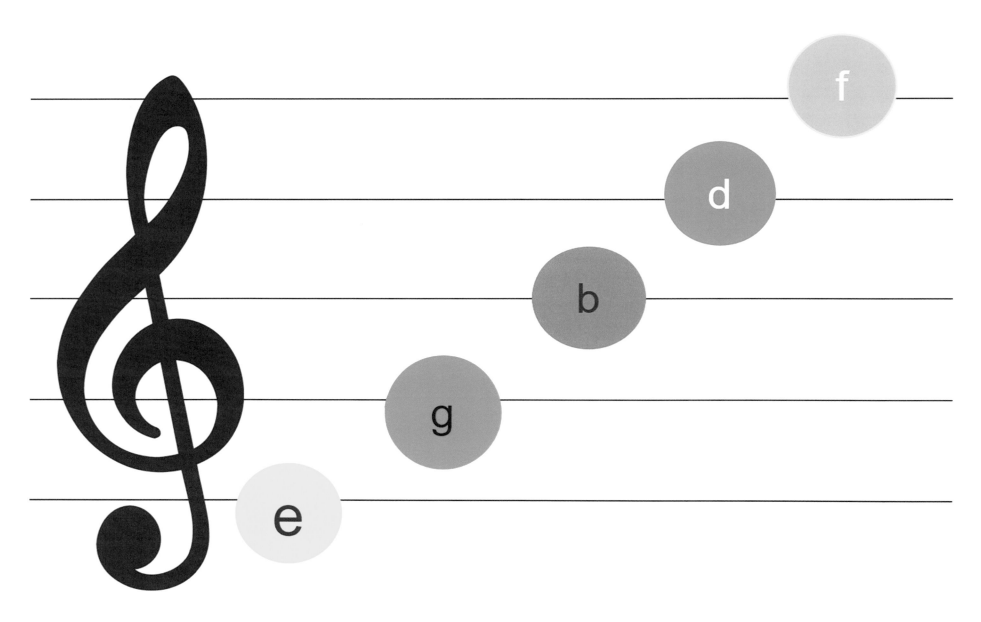

Figure 6.1b Treble clef with coloured notes

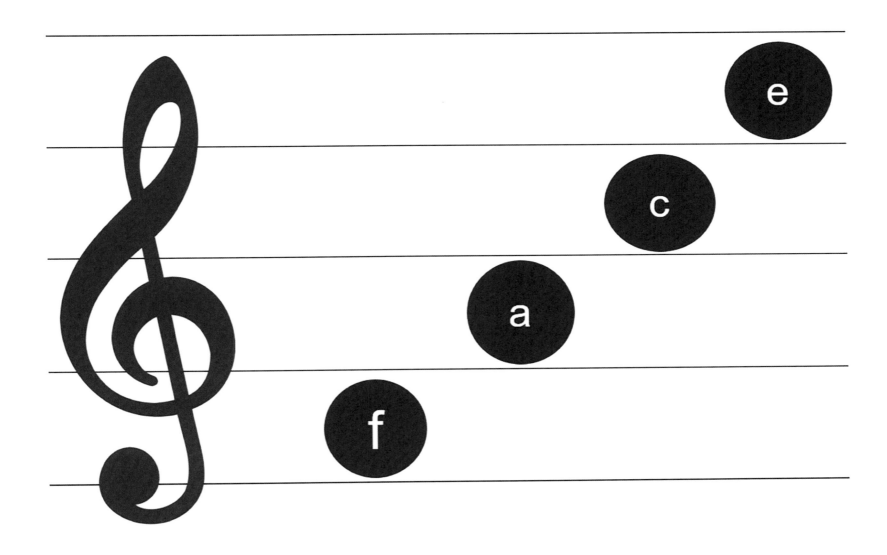

Figure 6.1c Treble clef with black notes

6. Using colour

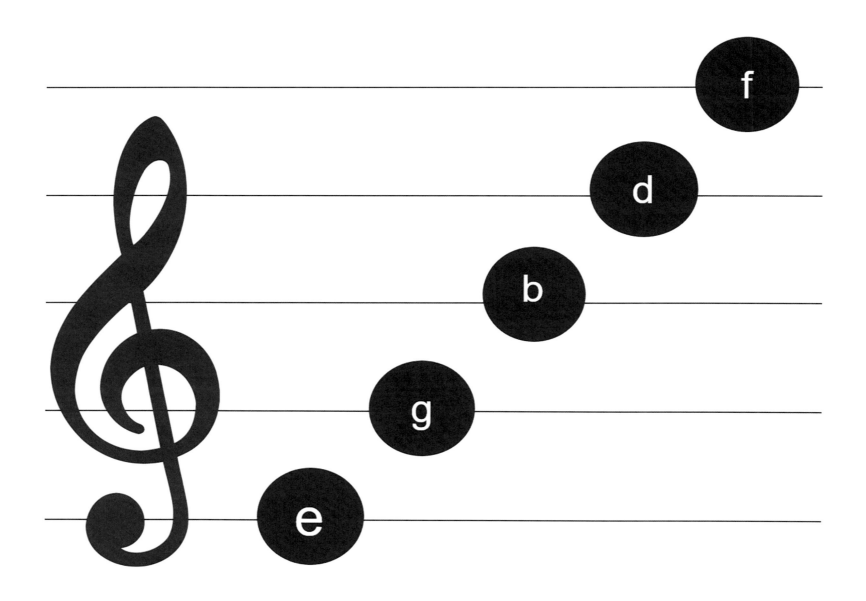

Figure 6.1d Treble clef with black notes

Figure 6.1e Treble clef with picture notes

6. Using colour

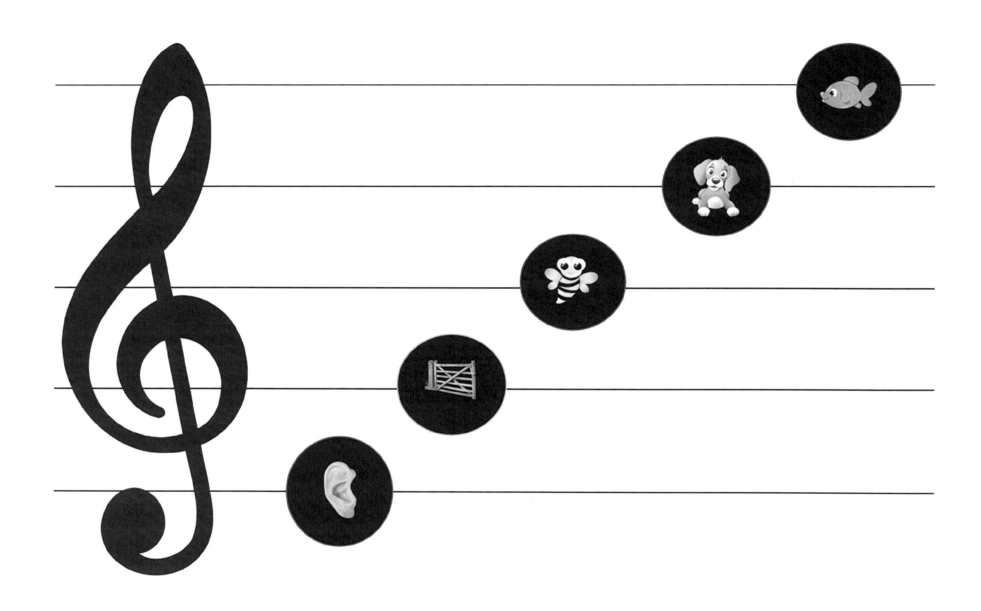

Figure 6.1f Treble clef with picture notes

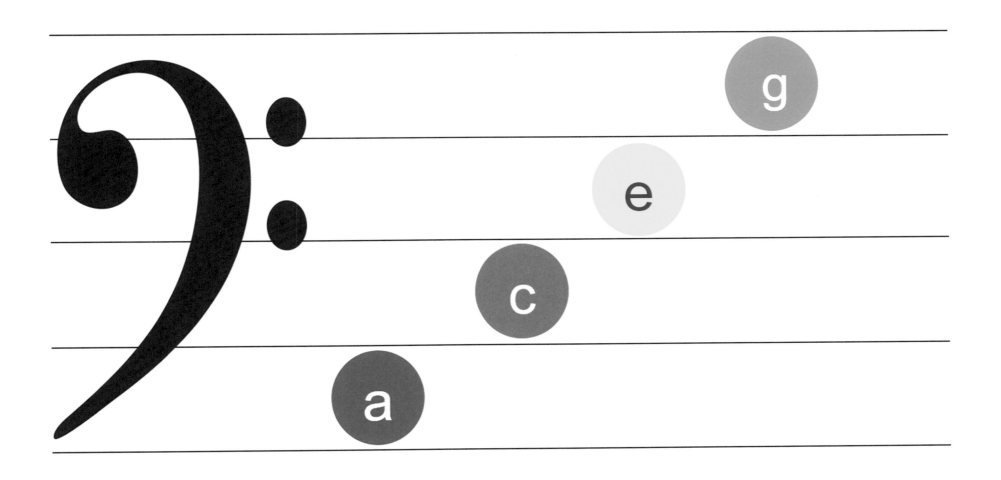

Figure 6.1g Bass clef with coloured notes

6. Using colour

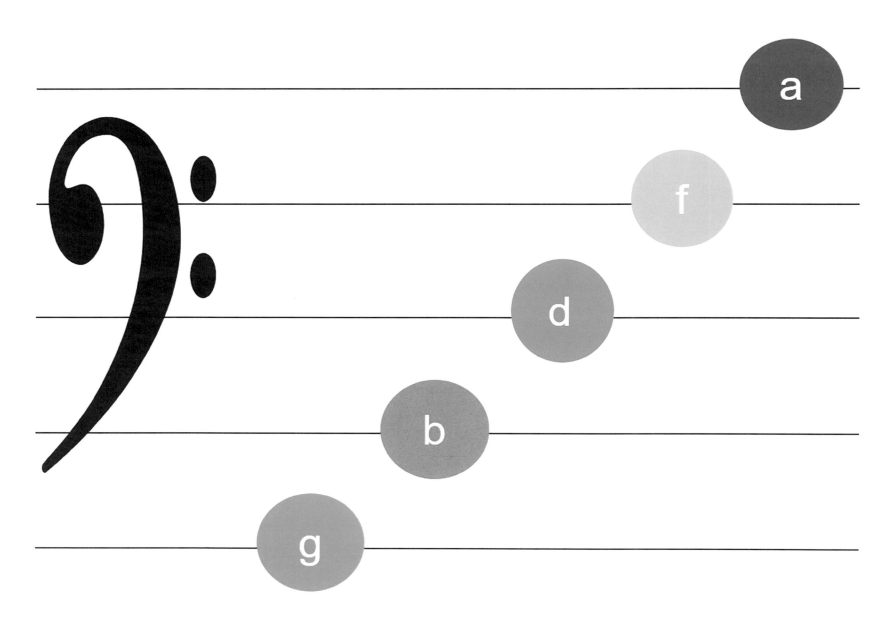

Figure 6.1h Bass clef with coloured notes

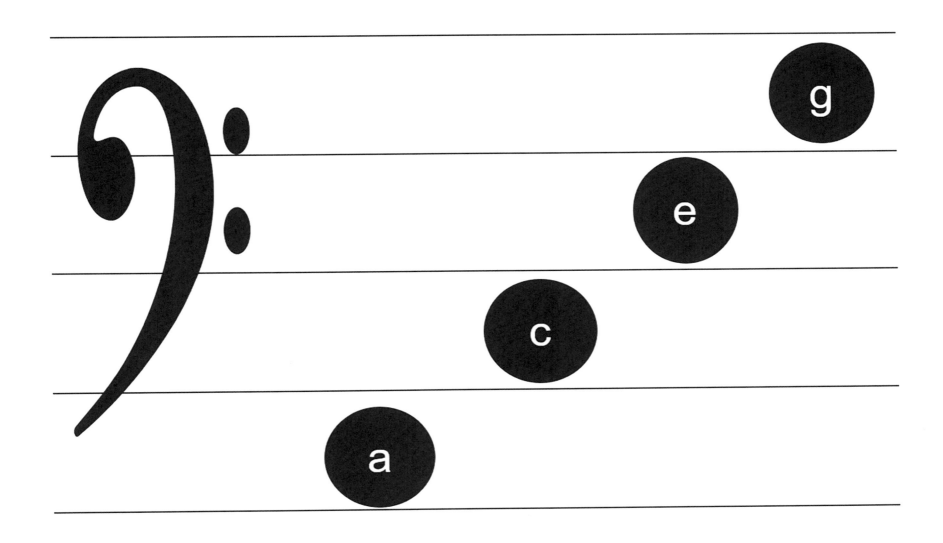

Figure 6.1i Bass clef with black notes

6. Using colour

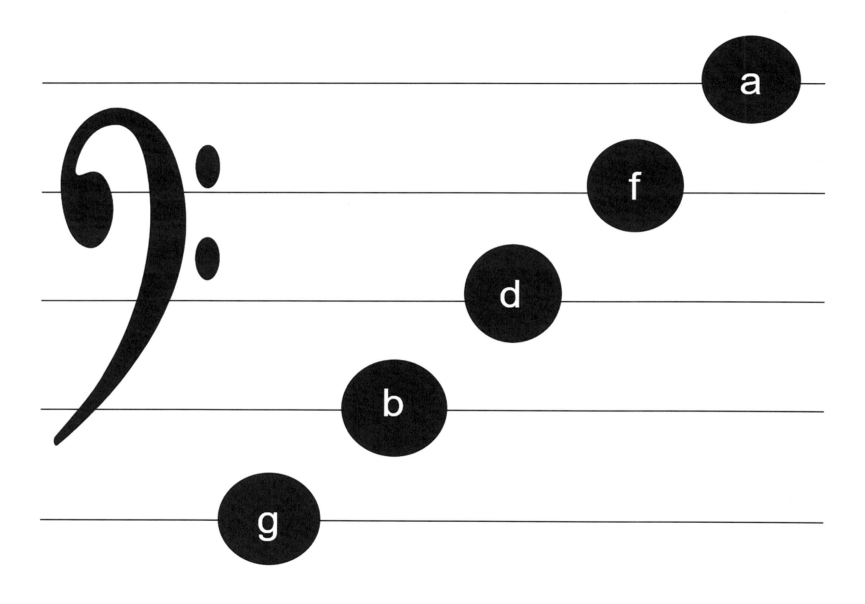

Figure 6.1j Bass clef with black notes

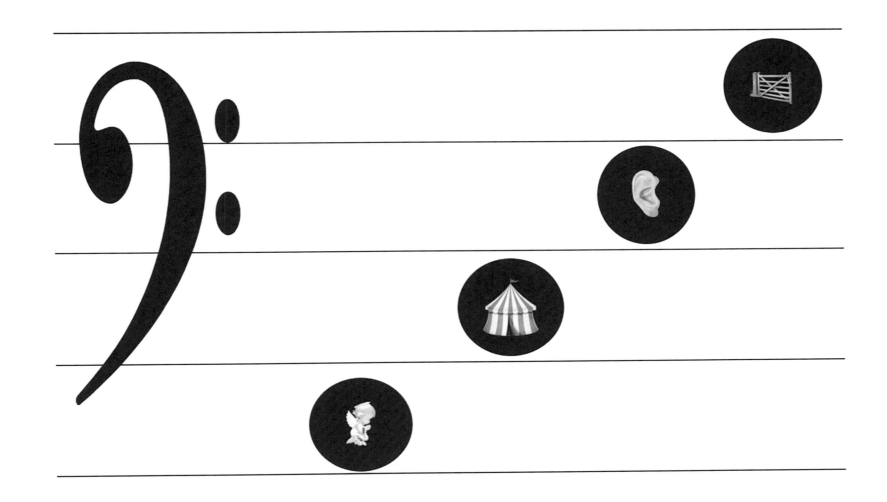

Figure 6.1k Bass clef with picture notes

Figure 6.1l Bass clef with picture notes

To help my younger students understand the placement of the notes on a stave and to introduce them to two of the components of a music score I give them 5 equal lengths of ribbon, about 1.5 metres long (you can buy ribbon cheaply from the sale box at any craft shop). I get them to place the 5 lengths of ribbon on the floor, in a straight line, about 8 inches apart to make the stave. I then ask them to cut out 8 foam circles (these can be bought online very reasonably), in the colours shown in Figure 6.2. I then ask my students to place the notes in the correct position and add the stems (which I have already cut out for them). Finally, I ask them to place the correct note name against the note foam circle they have put in place. Obviously, I provide a template for them to follow, as in Figure 6.2.

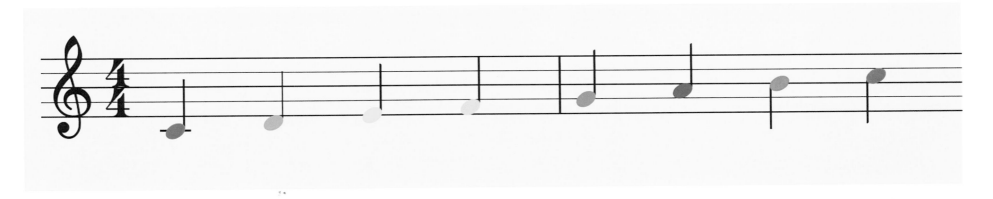

Figure 6.2 Template for placing notes using ribbon and foam

COLOURED STAVES

Coloured staves can also assist the dyslexic student to read music with greater ease, I always experiment with my students to see if they prefer coloured staves and, if they do, I initially work with them using a coloured stave. We carry out exercises using coloured and black staves and eventually (depending on their levels of confidence and anxiety) I slowly encourage them to transfer over to working with black staves. The advantage of working with coloured staves initially is that your student will get a better sense of where the note sits within the stave. Why? Because they will be able to differentiate between the colour of the note and the colour of the line of the stave far more easily.

Figures 6.3a–3e show examples of coloured staves which you can create quite easily on a computer. Initially, you can also get your student to draw the lines themselves, which will help them to understand that there are 5 lines within the stave, and which line the note sits on or between. I just start with the standard EGBDF and FACE patterns.

I had a student who found that upsizing the music to 150% resolved many of his issues. However, even with tinted glasses he still found that the lines of the staves blurred, unless they were set at 800% larger than the original score. Making the stave a different colour resolved this problem Why not copy the examples in Figures 6.3a–e and show your student? You can then assess whether they prefer using the coloured or the black staves. I have supplied the coloured staves in different colours and sizes and on different backgrounds.

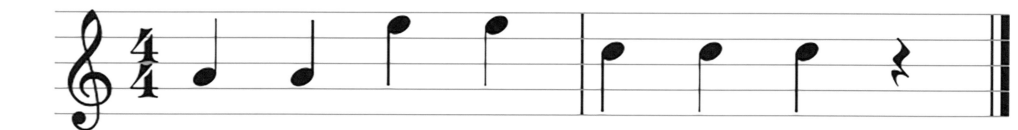

Figure 6.3a Green staves, two sizes

Figure 6.3b Pink staves, two sizes

6. Using colour

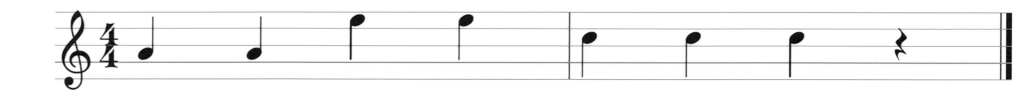

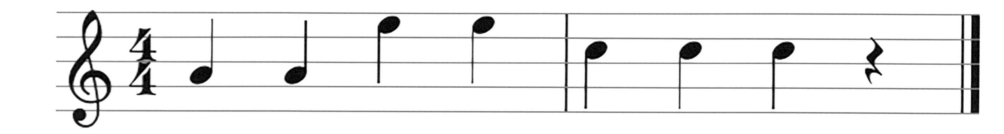

Figure 6.3c Orange staves, two sizes

Figure 6.3d Blue staves, two sizes

BAR LINES

Because some dyslexics can have considerable difficulty with spatial awareness, rests and bar lines can be a real issue. Several of my students have said they really wish that there were no bar lines in music.

One of the things that I have found particularly useful is changing the colour of the bar line within the music score

Figures 6.4a–4c are examples that can be shown to students to see if it makes a difference to them. You may need to make the bar lines a bit thicker. I normally go through the music my students are learning and mark the bar lines with a highlighter, which works just as well.

Dido's Lament

Purcell

Figure 6.4a Orange bar lines

6. Using colour

Dido's Lament

Purcell

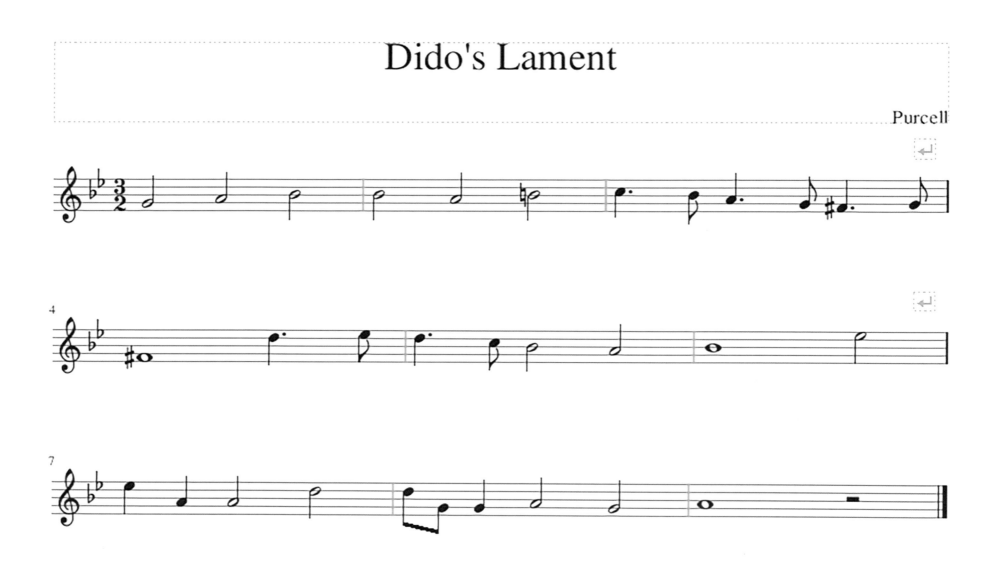

Figure 6.4b Green bar lines

Dido's Lament

Purcell

Figure 6.4c Pink bar lines

47

6. Using colour

As stated above, when a student is dyslexic all the components within a music score can blur or move around. Your student can find it almost impossible to separate each component, especially if they are all the same colour.

Occasionally, I have had to provide a copy of the score with the clef, key signature, time signature and dynamic markings in different colours. I initially Tippex over each marking and then replace them with handwritten coloured components (you have to be neat, and sadly that is not a gift I naturally have). I then photocopy the music so that the new coloured components present neatly (see Figure 6.4d).

If the music is not too complex, I have prepared it for my student on the computer. If you discuss what you are doing with your student, you can choose the colours that work best for them. Just a gentle reminder, all the current research indicates that you need to use low contrast colours (for further information see the section on fonts). Having found the combination of colours that works for your student, do not change them. If they know that the clef is blue and the time signature is green, they can focus on that one component, work out the instruction within the music score and then repeat the process with the other components you have marked up.

Figure 6.4d Coloured dynamic markings

6. Using colour

MUSIC STEM POSITIONS

Many dyslexic students have difficulty with coping with music stems going up or down. When teaching them instrumental music or theory, especially for the early exams at Grades 1, 2 and 3, I have adjusted the music so that the stems go in one direction. I'm afraid it means getting out the Tippex again or, if you have the skills, creating the music on a computer. It can make such a difference. As one of my younger students said to me, 'Ooooh, that is so much better.'

One of the simplest things you can do is to show your student a piece of music written in the normal manner (stems in both directions), and then the same piece of music with the stems in one direction. Your student will tell you which version they prefer. Figures 6.5a–5h are examples of comparative music scores so that you can ask your student which they prefer.

Dido's Lament normal music notes stem position

Purcell

Figure 6.5a Normal music note stems on yellow

6. Using colour

Dido's Lament music note stems in one direction

Purcell

Figure 6.5b Music note stems in one direction on yellow

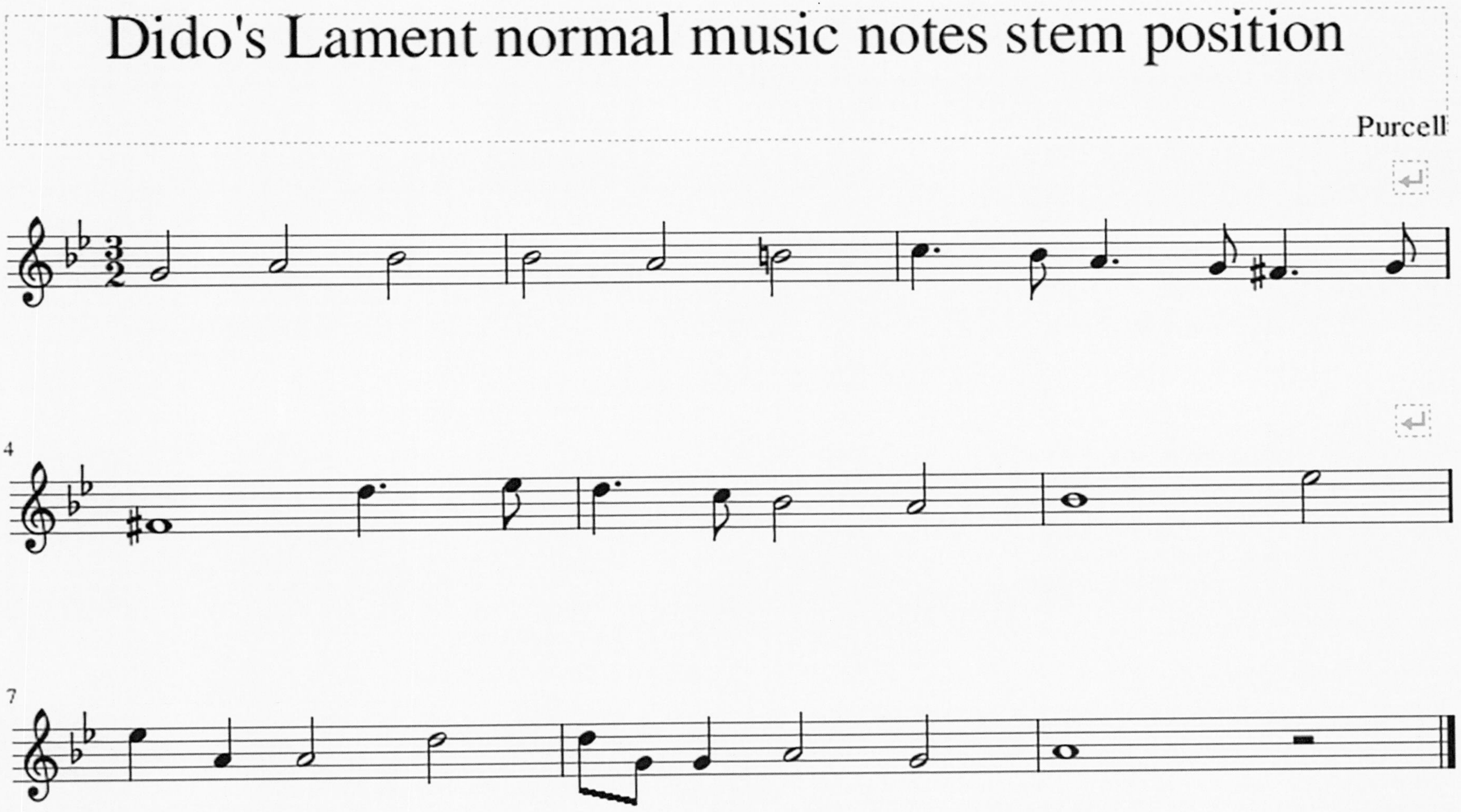

Figure 6.5c Normal music note stems on blue

6. Using colour

Figure 6.5d Music note stems in one direction on blue

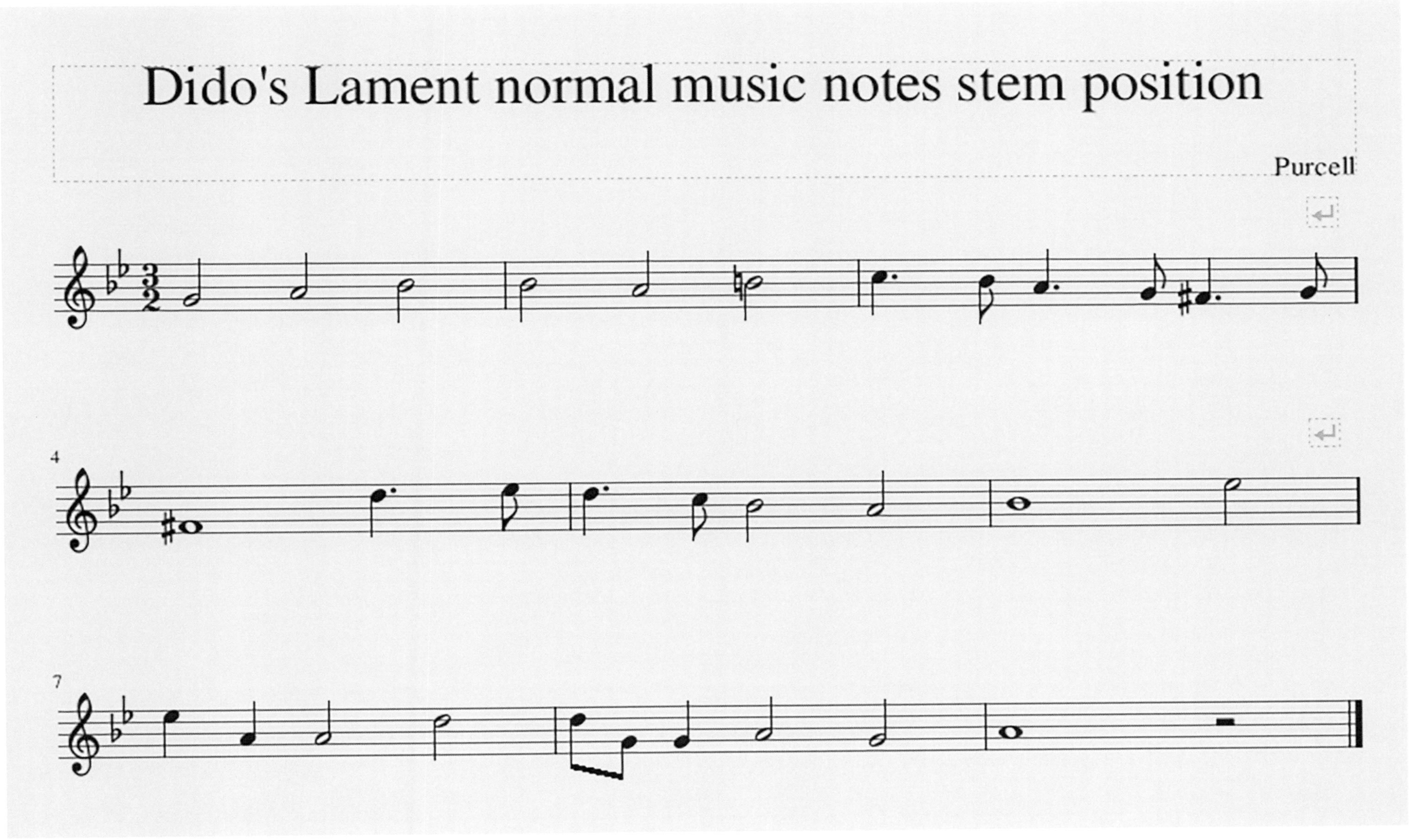

Dido's Lament normal music notes stem position

Purcell

Figure 6.5e Normal music note stems on pink

Dido's Lament music note stems in one direction

Purcell

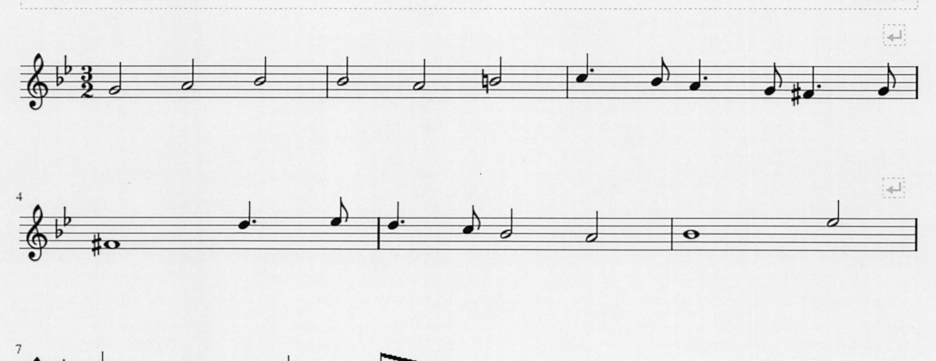

Figure 6.5f Music note stems in one direction on pink

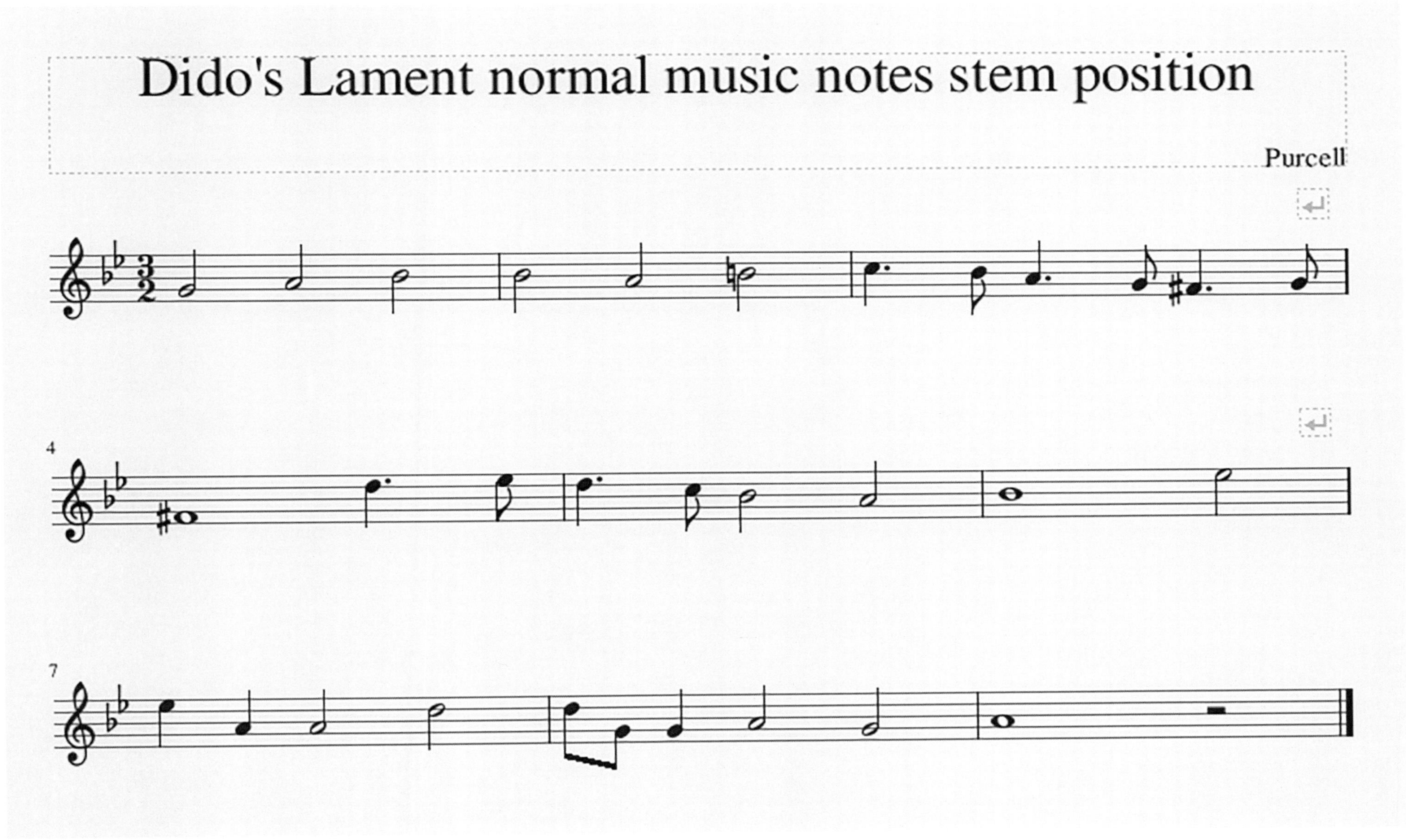

Figure 6.5g Normal music note stems on lilac

6. Using colour

Figure 6.5h Music note stems in one direction on lilac

FONTS

Research has shown that high contrast colours between text/music and paper (i.e. black text on a white background) can cause reading difficulties for dyslexic students.

It is accepted that dyslexics read better when text/music is presented on low contrast colours. The most recent research seems to indicate that many dyslexics prefer a yellow background with either blue or black text.

Further research has shown that larger font sizes and larger character spacings significantly improve readability for people with dyslexia. Specific fonts that have been found to aid the dyslexic student with reading are Courier, Arial and Verdana. That is why this book uses an Arial font.

Once again, I wanted to test this information out for myself. I showed my students different combinations of text with recommended fonts, spacing, colour and coloured paper scores. I found that there is no one combination of colours or font that works best for all my students. Again, this was a personal preference and each student chose a different combination. However, when you get the right combination it can make a significant difference. One of my students said there was a 60% improvement in her ability to read music and text after I introduced her to one of the Dyslexie Font combinations shown in Figures 6.7–6.9.

Figures 6.6a–6g provide a combination of background colours with contrasting text colours and fonts so that you and your students can explore which one offers the greatest assistance in reducing their visual stress.

Arial

Music can inspire, it can lift the soul to the very edge of heaven, free the mind and allow imagination to take flight. It calms and soothes the anxious mind, instantly reminds me of happy days, good friends, and good times. It gives life to everything and without it I am only partially alive.

Courier New

Music can inspire, it can lift the soul to the very edge of heaven, free the mind and allow imagination to take flight. It calms and soothes the anxious mind, instantly reminds me of happy days, good friends, and good times. It gives life to everything and without it I am only partially alive.

Verdana

Music can inspire, it can lift the soul to the very edge of heaven, free the mind and allow imagination to take flight. It calms and soothes the anxious mind, instantly reminds me of happy days, good friends, and good times. It gives life to everything and without it I am only partially alive.

Figure 6.6a Brown fonts on grey paper

Arial

Music can inspire, it can lift the soul to the very edge of heaven, free the mind and allow imagination to take flight. It calms and soothes the anxious mind, instantly reminds me of happy days, good friends, and good times. It gives life to everything and without it I am only partially alive.

Courier New

Music can inspire, it can lift the soul to the very edge of heaven, free the mind and allow imagination to take flight. It calms and soothes the anxious mind, instantly reminds me of happy days, good friends, and good times. It gives life to everything and without it I am only partially alive.

Verdana

Music can inspire, it can lift the soul to the very edge of heaven, free the mind and allow imagination to take flight. It calms and soothes the anxious mind, instantly reminds me of happy days, good friends, and good times. It gives life to everything and without it I am only partially alive.

Figure 6.6b Blue fonts on grey paper

6. Using colour

Arial

Music can inspire, it can lift the soul to the very edge of heaven, free the mind and allow imagination to take flight. It calms and soothes the anxious mind, instantly reminds me of happy days, good friends, and good times. It gives life to everything and without it I am only partially alive.

Courier New

Music can inspire, it can lift the soul to the very edge of heaven, free the mind and allow imagination to take flight. It calms and soothes the anxious mind, instantly reminds me of happy days, good friends, and good times. It gives life to everything and without it I am only partially alive.

Verdana

Music can inspire, it can lift the soul to the very edge of heaven, free the mind and allow imagination to take flight. It calms and soothes the anxious mind, instantly reminds me of happy days, good friends, and good times. It gives life to everything and without it I am only partially alive.

Figure 6.6c Blue fonts on pink paper

Arial

Music can inspire, it can lift the soul to the very edge of heaven, free the mind and allow imagination to take flight. It calms and soothes the anxious mind, instantly reminds me of happy days, good friends, and good times. It gives life to everything and without it I am only partially alive.

Courier New

Music can inspire, it can lift the soul to the very edge of heaven, free the mind and allow imagination to take flight. It calms and soothes the anxious mind, instantly reminds me of happy days, good friends, and good times. It gives life to everything and without it I am only partially alive.

Verdana

Music can inspire, it can lift the soul to the very edge of heaven, free the mind and allow imagination to take flight. It calms and soothes the anxious mind, instantly reminds me of happy days, good friends, and good times. It gives life to everything and without it I am only partially alive.

Figure 6.6d Brown fonts on yellow paper

Arial

Music can inspire, it can lift the soul to the very edge of heaven, free the mind and allow imagination to take flight. It calms and soothes the anxious mind, instantly reminds me of happy days, good friends, and good times. It gives life to everything and without it I am only partially alive.

Courier New

Music can inspire, it can lift the soul to the very edge of heaven, free the mind and allow imagination to take flight. It calms and soothes the anxious mind, instantly reminds me of happy days, good friends, and good times. It gives life to everything and without it I am only partially alive.

Verdana

Music can inspire, it can lift the soul to the very edge of heaven, free the mind and allow imagination to take flight. It calms and soothes the anxious mind, instantly reminds me of happy days, good friends, and good times. It gives life to everything and without it I am only partially alive.

Figure 6.6e Black fonts on yellow paper

Arial

Music can inspire, it can lift the soul to the very edge of heaven, free the mind and allow imagination to take flight. It calms and soothes the anxious mind, instantly reminds me of happy days, good friends, and good times. It gives life to everything and without it I am only partially alive.

Courier New

Music can inspire, it can lift the soul to the very edge of heaven, free the mind and allow imagination to take flight. It calms and soothes the anxious mind, instantly reminds me of happy days, good friends, and good times. It gives life to everything and without it I am only partially alive.

Verdana

Music can inspire, it can lift the soul to the very edge of heaven, free the mind and allow imagination to take flight. It calms and soothes the anxious mind, instantly reminds me of happy days, good friends, and good times. It gives life to everything and without it I am only partially alive.

Figure 6.6f Brown fonts on blue paper

Arial

Music can inspire, it can lift the soul to the very edge of heaven, free the mind and allow imagination to take flight. It calms and soothes the anxious mind, instantly reminds me of happy days, good friends, and good times. It gives life to everything and without it I am only partially alive.

Courier New

Music can inspire, it can lift the soul to the very edge of heaven, free the mind and allow imagination to take flight. It calms and soothes the anxious mind, instantly reminds me of happy days, good friends, and good times. It gives life to everything and without it I am only partially alive.

Verdana

Music can inspire, it can lift the soul to the very edge of heaven, free the mind and allow imagination to take flight. It calms and soothes the anxious mind, instantly reminds me of happy days, good friends, and good times. It gives life to everything and without it I am only partially alive.

Figure 6.6g Blue fonts on yellow paper

Dyslexie Font has been created specifically for dyslexics by Christian Boer, who is dyslexic himself. He has kindly given me permission to share some examples of the font and text adjustments in this book. Researchers who have studied the benefits of Dyslexie Font are divided in their opinion as to whether it is an effective aid in enhancing a dyslexic's ability to read, but 75% of my students have indicated at least a 50% improvement when we explored the various combinations of colour and spacing. Some of my students now use it for their schoolwork and general reading. I have provided some examples of Dyslexie Font combinations in Figures 6.7–6.9 – examples of all the combinations would take a whole book. You can subscribe to Dyslexie Font at a reasonable monthly fee. You can sign up to a trial period, so you can explore all the possible combinations – www.dyslexiefont.com/

EXAMPLES OF DYSLEXIE FONT – ENLARGED

Mr Rabbit leaned against the wall and looked at the carrots in Farmer Brown's field and asked himself "umm I wonder how many of those carrots I could eat"

Figure 6.7a Dyslexie – enlarged

Mr Rabbit leaned against the wall and looked at the carrots in Farmer Brown's field and asked himself "umm I wonder how many of those carrots I could eat"

Figure 6.7b Dyslexie – enlarged

Mr Rabbit leaned against the wall and looked at the carrots in Farmer Brown's field and asked himself "umm I wonder how many of those carrots I could eat"

Figure 6.7c Dyslexie – enlarged

EXAMPLES OF DYSLEXIE FONT– INCREASED LINE SPACING

Mr Rabbit leaned against the wall and looked at the carrots in Farmer Brown's field and asked himself "umm I wonder how many of those carrots I could eat"

Figure 6.8a Dyslexie – increased line spacing

Mr Rabbit leaned against the wall and looked at the

carrots in Farmer Brown's field and asked himself "umm

I wonder how many of those carrots I could eat"

Figure 6.8b Dyslexie – increased line spacing

Mr Rabbit leaned against the wall and looked at the

carrots in Farmer Brown's field and asked himself "umm

I wonder how many of those carrots I could eat"

Figure 6.8c Dyslexie – increased line spacing

EXAMPLES OF DYSLEXIE FONT – INCREASED WORD SPACING

Mr Rabbit leaned against the wall and looked at the carrots in

Farmer Brown's field and asked himself "ummm I wonder how many

of those carrots I could eat"

Figure 6.9a Dyslexie – increased word spacing

Mr Rabbit leaned against the wall and looked at the carrots in Farmer Brown's field and asked himself "umm I wonder how many of those carrots I could eat"

Figure 6.9b Dyslexie – increased word spacing

Mr Rabbit leaned against the wall and looked at the carrots in Farmer Brown's field and asked himself "umm I wonder how many of those carrots I could eat"

Figure 6.9c Dyslexie – increased word spacing

6. Using colour

I have also used Open Dyslexic, which provides different typefaces to assist dyslexics, but because of copyright issues I cannot show you examples. More information is at https://www.dafont.com/open-dyslexic.font.

I always prepare mock exam papers for my students and I have found that discovering which font works best for a dyslexic student makes a significant difference to their ability to revise. Exploring fonts with your students will help you to understand:

1. Which font reduces visual stress most effectively
2. Which font size reduces visual stress most effectively
3. What combination of paper colour against text colour works most effectively
4. Which font has the best character spacing that works most successfully
5. Whether the text line spacing needs to be adjusted.

It is so uplifting to show a student several fonts and, when they see the one that reduces their visual stress, to hear them say in a surprised voice, 'That really makes a difference. I don't know how, but it really makes a difference.'

DYNAMIC MARKINGS

Dynamic markings are yet another component within a music score. Quite a few students don't actually register the markings when presented with a score, and I have had to point them out . I use a highlighter to emphasise the dynamic markings. I agree a colour with my student, and they know that if they see that colour there is a dynamic mark and they need to concentrate so that they can note what the marking is.

RESTS

Because rests present a spatial anomaly, they can cause a dyslexic student to become anxious and panicky as many of them don't see the rest but see a space. As there appears to be no reason for the space this can cause considerable stress. For example, I was demonstrating how to sing 'Electricity', the student sang back the first section of music, but on the second section I could hear panic in their voice and the rhythm was incorrect. Here is a section of the conversation that took place between us:

Me *'Can you see the notes, X?'*

X *'Yes, but I don't understand what is happening.'*

Me *'Explain what you don't understand.'*

X *'This bit doesn't make sense, there is a gap.'*

Me *'Can you see that little mark?'*

X *'Yes.'*

Me *'That is a dotted quaver rest. So, let's look at the value of the notes you are singing ...'*

I have found that if I explain why spaces appear in the music, most students will quickly take the reason on board. They are then able to adjust their thinking to accommodate the necessity for the space. If they cannot see the rest (which can be rather small) they learn to count the notes that they can see and then they can work out the value of the rest, which is in the space.

CHECKLIST

1. Have you upsized the music score you are working on with your student?
2. Have you explored whether your student prefers the music score printed on different coloured paper?
3. Have you experimented with the visual overlays to see if your student has a preference?
4. Have you asked your student if they prefer coloured notes or black notes?
5. Have you asked your student if they prefer coloured staves?
6. Have you investigated whether your student prefers coloured bar lines or black bar lines?
7. Have you explored with your student whether they prefer the music stems in the normal position or all going in the same direction?
8. Have you noticed whether your student gets anxious or panicky when they see a rest?
9. Have you discerned whether your student can actually see all the dynamic markings on a music score?
10. Have you explored if your student prefers using a particular font when reading lyrics?
11. Have you examined whether your student prefers to use Dyslexie Font?

Writing music can also present difficulties for the dyslexic music student as many of them also have dysgraphia. Dysgraphia is typified by difficulties in writing and was defined by the American Psychiatric Association in 1994 as a disorder of written expression which is typified by

> writing skills (that) ... are substantially below those expected given the person's chronological age, measured intelligence, and age-appropriate education.

There is an ongoing debate as to whether dysgraphia is caused by an impairment of the cerebellum in the brain, by phonological processing or by magnocellular processing (all of which I talk about later). However, at the present time the argument that dysgraphia is caused by an impairment in the cerebellum (see Figure 7.1) is gaining a little more ground. This is because it has been proven that the cerebellum plays a critical role in the first stages of sequence learning. It is also acknowledged that the striatum, which is a nucleus in the subcortical basal ganglia of the forebrain, is essential for the later stages of learning.

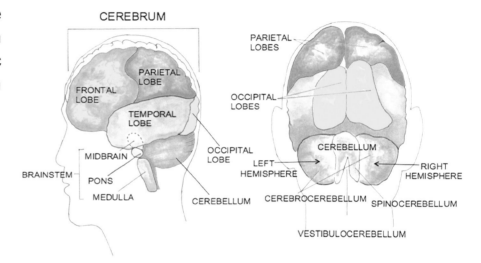

Figure 7.1 Dysgraphia

Impairments in the function of these two parts of the brain have been shown to undermine a person's ability to learn because of their critical involvement in skill learning and skill automaticity. It has been accepted for some time that repeated automatic acts can result in the human brain reorganising itself. This has been evidenced by studies undertaken on taxi drivers learning 'The Knowledge' (Jabr, 2011). It has also been proven that intensive training in an area such as music can produce long-lasting functional and structural modifications in the brain (Wan and Schlaug, 2010; Herholz and Zatorre, 2012). Automaticity can change the plasticity within the brain and, although there are other theories on what causes dysgraphia, in this book I am going to concentrate on the need to improve automaticity in dyslexic/dysgraphic students.

WRITING MUSIC

To assess whether there is a problem with a student's ability to write music I provide them with ordinary sheet music (upsized) and ask them to copy down a section of music. It soon becomes obvious if the student is having difficulty with this task.

There are various aids that enable the dyslexic student to write music, including specialised pens and pencils for dysgraphics. These are easily available and an online search will show you where to buy them. Your student may already be using specialised pens if they have been diagnosed with dysgraphia. Don't forget to ask if they use them for their schoolwork. If they do, remind them to use them when they are writing music. As every child is different it is likely that each student may find a different specialist pen/pencil easier to write with. Again, just experiment until you find the one that works best for your student.

Some studies have provided an insight into how people acquire new skills. In 1964, Fitts explained that there were three stages to this process:

- *When a person is introduced to a new task it requires their repeated involvement and training to initially learn the task. For example, when I began driving, I couldn't distinguish between my brake and my accelerator. I had to be taught what each component of the car should be used for, and when they should be used. The more driving lessons I had the more I improved. Eventually I understood what all the elements inside the car were for and when to use them. As a result, I completed the first stage of the learning process.*

- *The second stage of learning takes more time to acquire. As an individual continually practises and repeats the tasks that are required to acquire a new skill their ability to perform the new skill is enhanced. The advantage with this stage of learning is the memory of the action required to complete the task becomes stronger and more embedded in the psyche. In this way there is consolidation of the knowledge that has been gained. So, returning to the driving analogy, do you remember a driving lesson where you got in the car, adjusted the mirror, checked that there was no other traffic near you, slipped into first gear and eased out of the parking space onto the road? I am sure that you were still nervous at this stage, but you had acquired all the knowledge you needed to drive!!!!*

• The third stage of learning occurs almost without conscious thought. It happens when an individual practises a task to perfect a skill. The more the task is practised the more they improve until they can perform the task automatically. As actions required to complete the task are memorised, the ability to perform that task is enhanced, becomes stronger and more embedded, until the task can be completed competently and, in many cases, automatically. Returning to the car analogy, when you get into your car now, don't you just put the car in gear and drive to wherever you need to go? You are not thinking 'Ooooh I must

remember to push down on the accelerator to drive faster' or 'Ooh I need to go slow here so I had better brake' or, 'I am driving above 40 so I need to be in 5th gear', instead you do all this automatically. You can be driving and thinking of something totally unrelated to driving and yet still be alert enough to be aware of other road user's actions.

As I explained at the beginning of this book, it is necessary to teach dyslexic music students using a multi-sensory approach. The repeated action of writing a music note will help your student to recognise the shape of a note, even if it is slightly blurry or is moving on the page.

Many dyslexics have difficulties with phonological issues including:

- Memory
- Word retrieval
- Verbal processing speeds.

When learning a new skill, such as how to write music, dyslexic students can find themselves in difficulty. They encounter problems, not only in trying to write music notes, but also in remembering how to write them. Some of the things dyslexic students have difficulties with are:

- Writing notes the right way around
- Remembering to add the music stem
- Remembering to colour in the note if it is a crochet or a quaver
- Remembering to add the tails for the quavers, semiquavers and so on
- Remembering where to place the notes on the stave
- Remembering the name of the note.

Part of the reason for this difficulty is that the third stage of acquiring a skill can be compromised by dyslexia. Why? Because the ability to gain automaticity when learning a task is dependent upon deeper memorisation of the actions required to complete that task. If a student has phonological difficulties that manifest in an inability to recall information, words or images with ease, they are going to face problems when trying to remember:

- Note names
- Note values
- Note positions on a stave, including writing notes back to front
- Note colours
- Note imagery
- Clef names.

This is where patience and enthusiasm can really come into play. Studies have shown that dyslexic students can improve their ability to learn a new skill by working on their automaticity ability through the use of drill and practice programmes and working memory tasks.

Really interesting work by Horowitz-Kraus and Brenitz in 2009 involved a word memory study. This required both dyslexics and non-dyslexics to engage in frequent working memory tasks that were visual, auditory and a combination of both. At the end of the training both dyslexics and non-dyslexic's memories had improved. However, some (not all) of the gains the dyslexic participants had made were lost because they did not continue with the tasks. Further studies have shown that with working memory tasks and consistent drill practice, dyslexic students' automaticity ability does improve.

CHECKLIST

1. Which two areas of the brain is it believed are most involved in being able to write?
2. What are the three stages of learning?
3. What area of learning is most impacted by dysgraphia?

4. What are the 6 things that are affected when a student with dysgraphia attempts to write music?
5. What might a student with dyslexia have difficulty remembering when writing music?
6. What method can you use to assist a dyslexic student in remembering how to write music?

IMPROVING AUTOMATICITY WHEN WRITING MUSIC

Repetition is important when teaching dyslexic/dysgraphic music students how to write music. Regular repetition exercises are yet another tool to help students remember:

- Which way the notes face
- That the majority of notes need a stem
- That crochets and quavers need to be coloured in
- That to create a quaver, semiquaver and so on, you need to add a tail
- The names of the clefs
- Note values
- That the direction of the stem is up or down and not to the side

- The appropriate size of the note, clef and so on, as some students will make the symbols too small or too big.

HOW BEST TO HELP IMPROVE AUTOMATICITY

One of the best ways I have found to help my students improve automaticity when they are writing music is by using music trace worksheets. Many versions can be accessed on the internet, but the ones I use constantly can be found at http://www.musicfun.net.au/worksheets.htm. They were created by Beatrice Wilder, an Australian music teacher, and my students love them. I get my students to cut out and colour the wonderful large notes Beatrice provides on her worksheets. This activity engages them kinaesthetically as they learn the shape of the notes by cutting them out, and the colour of the notes by colouring them in. In addition, the students are creating notes as they draw around the trace notes. These actions, undertaken regularly, are working memory tasks.

Repetition (and I know I am being repetitive) is a vital tool when assisting the dyslexic music student. You must be patient. Keep reminding them to colour in the note heads and to add the stems, until eventually they do it automatically. It will take longer to teach a dyslexic student this skill but once they have mastered writing the music notes, it is a skill learnt for life. Remember to use constant encouragement and praise throughout the lessons.

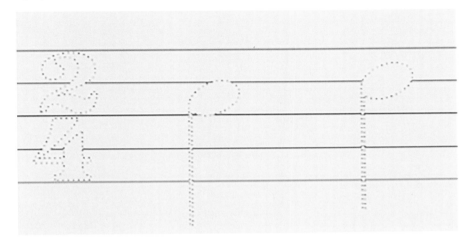

Figure 7.2 Music trace

The importance of encouraging students to do 10 minutes tracing or cutting out of notes, at least 5 times a week, should be explained to their parents and guardians. Students should be reminded to go through their music note trace sheets to:

1. Colour in the note heads for crochets and quavers
2. Add the stem to the music note
3. Write the notes the correct way around.

You will have to remind your students to do this many times. They will get there, and when they do you will get such a buzz from watching their confidence and self-esteem grow.

Tracing notes is great. However, I also found that positive results were obtained using a technique called 'Davis Symbol Mastery'. In this process students work with clay to create visual interpretations of a word's meaning. Students then connect those interpretations to the word's spelling and pronunciation. This is a multi-sensory approach to learning to spell. I loved the idea, so I adapted it and tested it on my students using plasticine.

I encouraged my students, when they were learning how to write music, to create notes and symbols out of plasticine. This gave them a three-dimensional sense of the notes and symbols. My students loved it and one of the many comments was, 'It helps you feel the shape of the note,' which helped them to visualise the note when they came to write it.

I then give my students a mini-score on paper and some plasticine and ask them to recreate the mini-score with the plasticine. The students will do this at my music studio. I also give them this task as homework. To ensure that it is done by them and no one else, I ask parents to take photographs of the student during various stages of creating the music score.

The method is simple:

1. Give the students an upsized simple music score (as supplied in Figures 7.3a–c)
2. Hand them a pack of black and white plasticine
3. Ask them to recreate the mini-score you have given them, including the clef sign, stave and notes.

Music score for creation of plasticine of notes

Figure 7.3a Score for plasticine creation of notes

Figure 7.3b Score for plasticine creation of notes

Figure 7.3c Score for plasticine creation of notes

You can go one stage further and ask your students to create the notes with air-drying modelling clay. They can then paint the crochets and quavers black, and the breves and minims black and white. This reinforces not only the shapes but also the colours of the notes.

CHECKLIST

1. Have you checked if any of your students are having difficulty writing music?
2. Have you pinpointed their particular difficulty (i.e. writing the note back to front)?
3. What three methods can you use to help improve your student's automaticity?

7. Dysgraphia

8. KINAESTHESIA AND DYSLEXIA

As you have seen, writing music and dealing with phonological issues are interlinked. Phonological issues not only result in problems with word retrieval and phonological processing, but also give rise to such issues as understanding rhythms. This is where kinaesthetic teaching will help. When teaching rhythm, I combine repetition with kinaesthetic reinforcement.

Research has shown that if a student has well developed physical coordination this assists with their cognitive functioning. This in turn impacts positively on their academic capabilities in reading, language and mathematics. These are all skills that are required when reading music. Research has also shown that areas of the brain in a dyslexic do not function in the same manner as someone who is non-dyslexic. This dysfunction can impact on the development of a student's physical coordination and academic skills. It can also give some dyslexics difficulty with word and memory retrieval. As musicians it causes problems with their ability to memorise rhythms and sequential patterns. Studies have found that visual cues prompt body movements in all children, while a dyslexic child's body movements have been found to be weaker and more erratic when compared with non-dyslexics. It is accepted that if a dyslexic's physical coordination is improved their academic ability also improves.

Remembering rhythms and note values can be a challenge for the dyslexic music student. I know from working with my students how frustrating they can find not being able to maintain their rhythm when learning a song/music. It is acknowledged that body percussive movements (clapping, tapping and stamping) assist with improving automaticity when learning rhythms. I can confirm that my dyslexic students' rhythm skills have improved as a result of engaging them in repeated and regular clapping and stamping exercises.

On the next few pages are various rhythm exercises I have created. Without fail, I spend 5–10 minutes of each lesson clapping rhythms with my dyslexic students. I also use clapping when a student has a problem with timing in a piece of music. I frequently teach parents/guardians the rhythms on the sheets so that they can play rhythm games with my students, it is fun for them. Why do I do this? Because without this constant repetition the automaticity that needs to be developed in the student cannot occur.

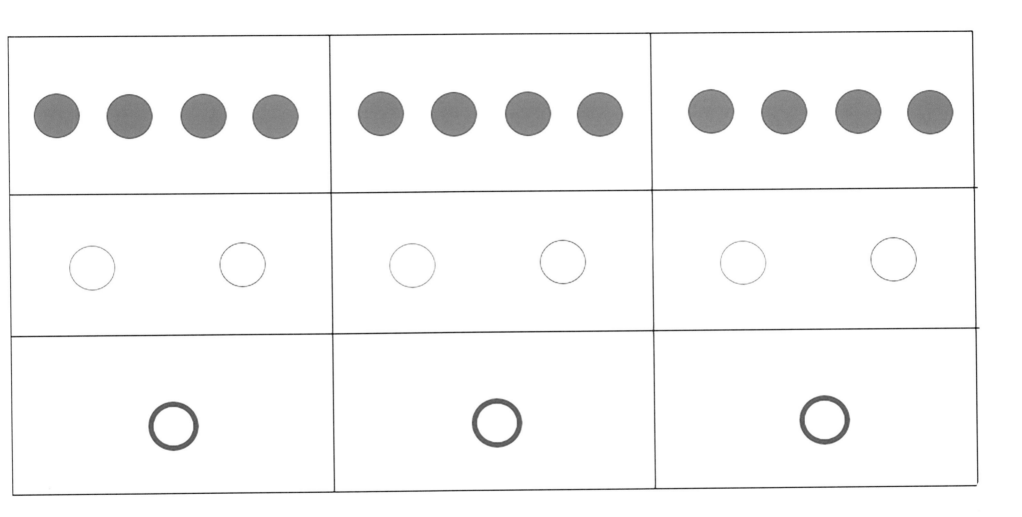

Figure 8.1a Rhythm exercise

8. Kinaesthesia and dyslexia

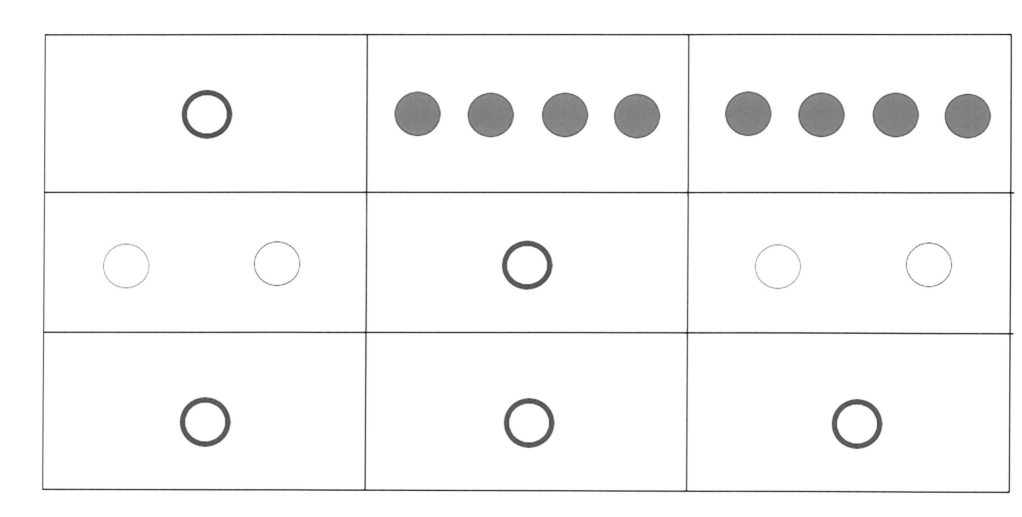

Figure 8.1b Rhythm exercise

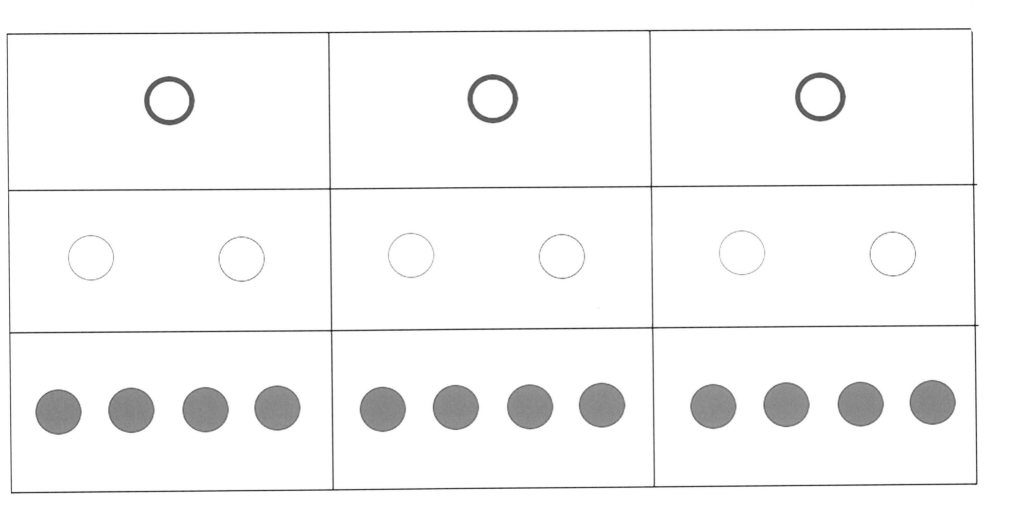

Figure 8.1c Rhythm exercise

8. Kinaesthesia and dyslexia

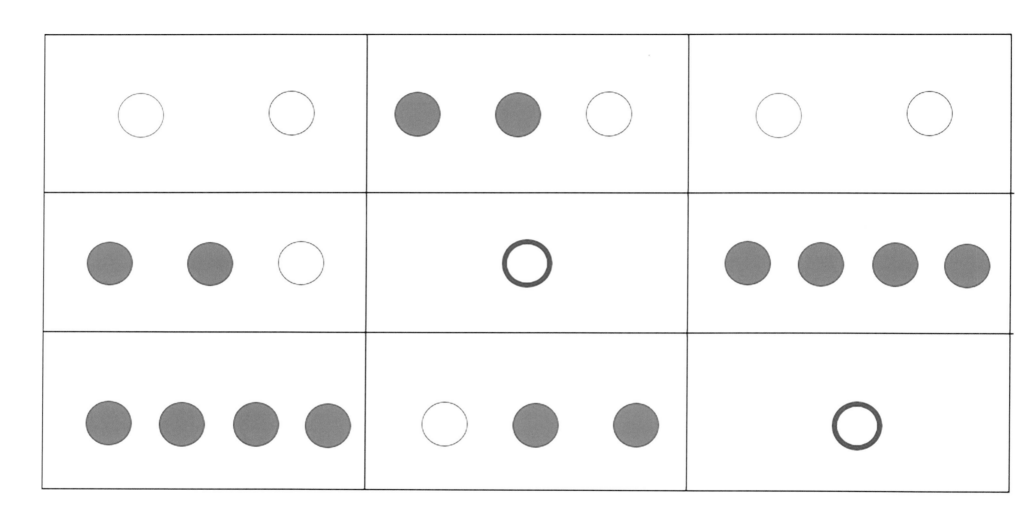

Figure 8.1d Rhythm exercise

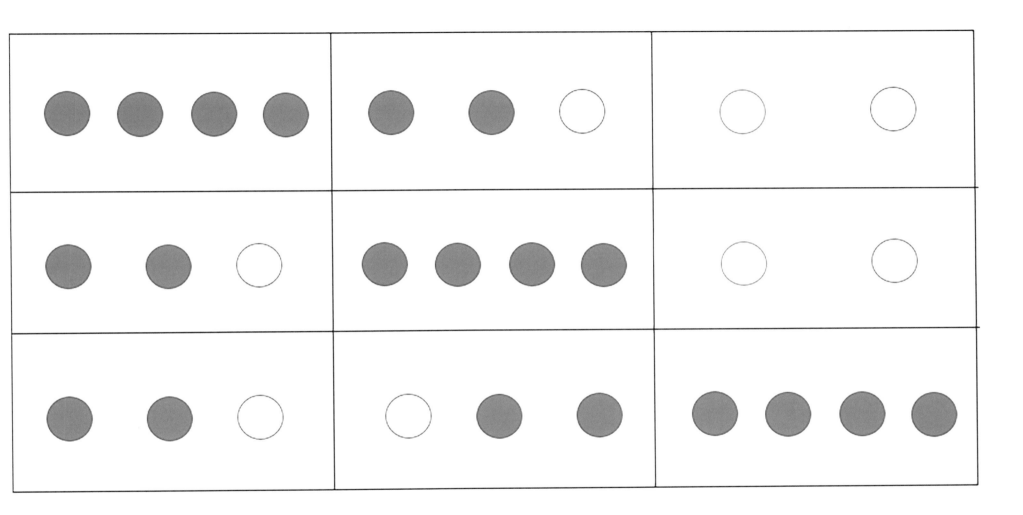

Figure 8.1e Rhythm exercise

8. Kinaesthesia and dyslexia

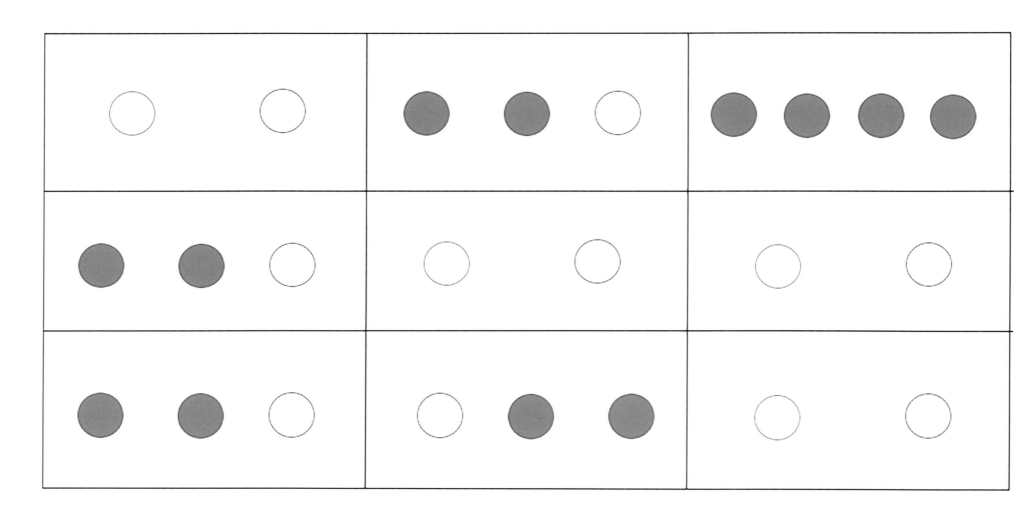

Figure 8.1f Rhythm exercise

8. Kinaesthesia and dyslexia
88

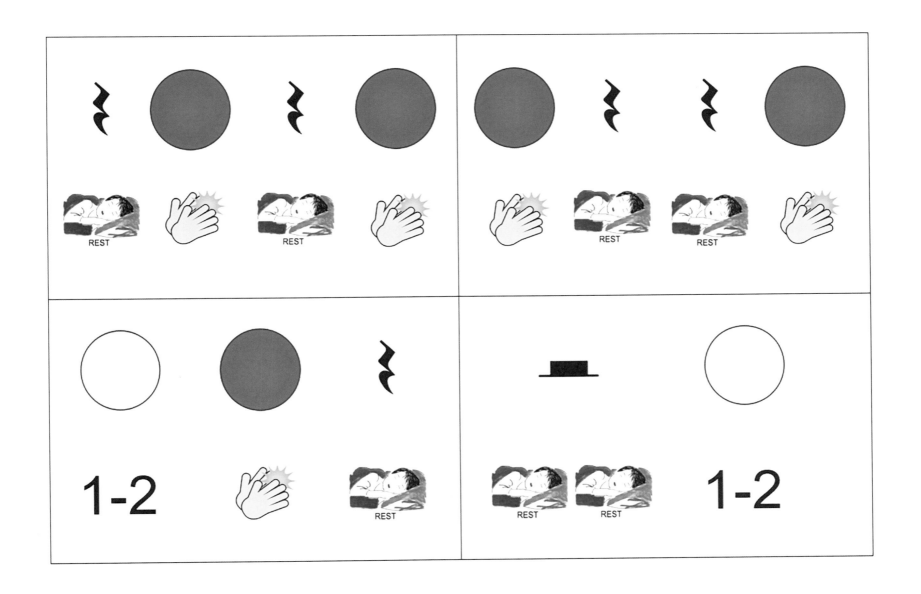

Figure 8.1g Rhythm exercise

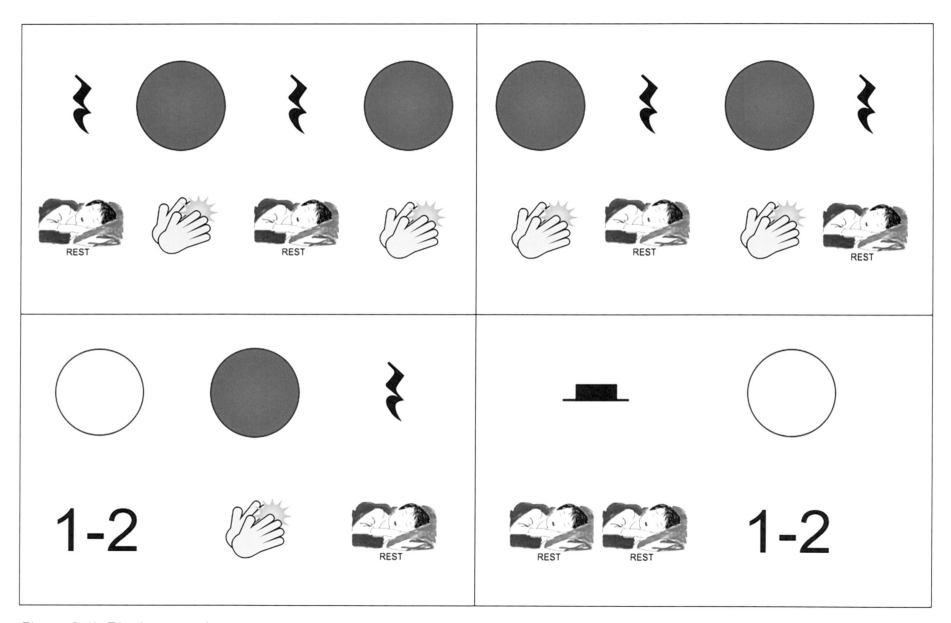

Figure 8.1h Rhythm exercise

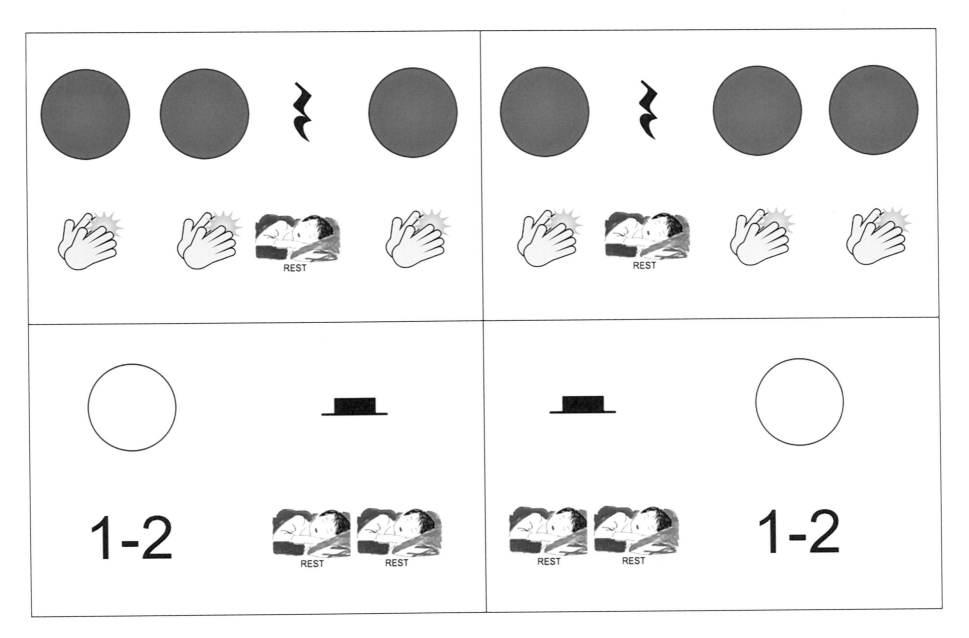

Figure 8.1i Rhythm exercise

8. Kinaesthesia and dyslexia

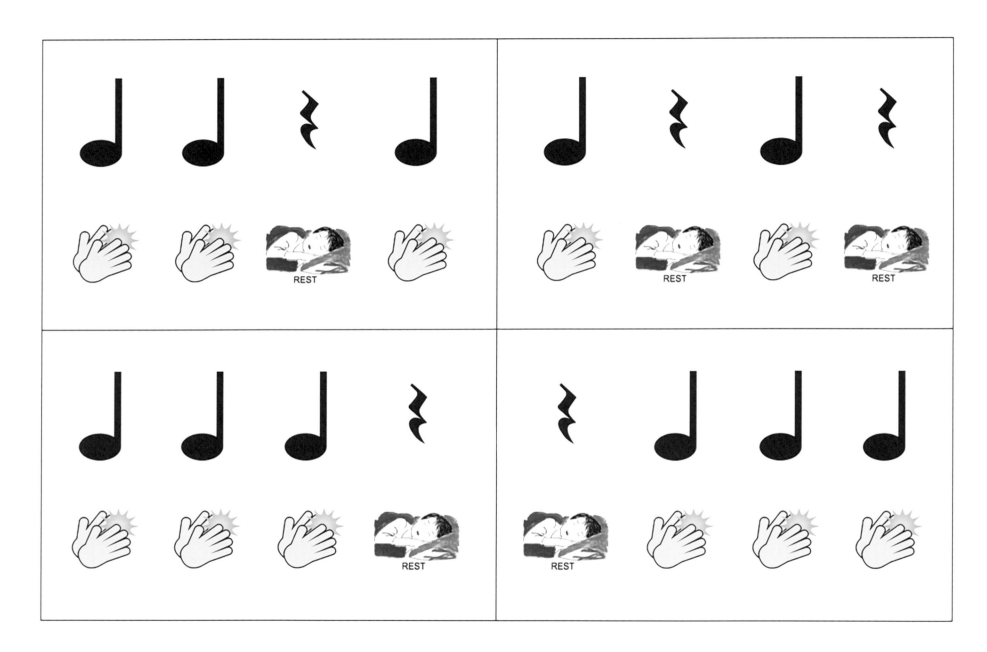

Figure 8.1j Rhythm exercise

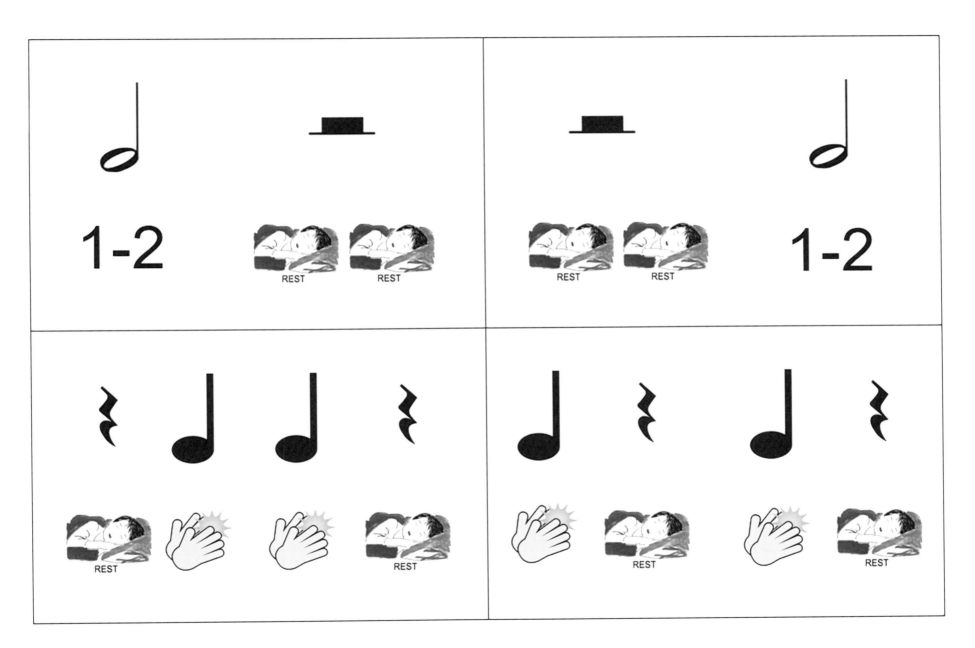

Figure 8.1k Rhythm exercise

8. Kinaesthesia and dyslexia

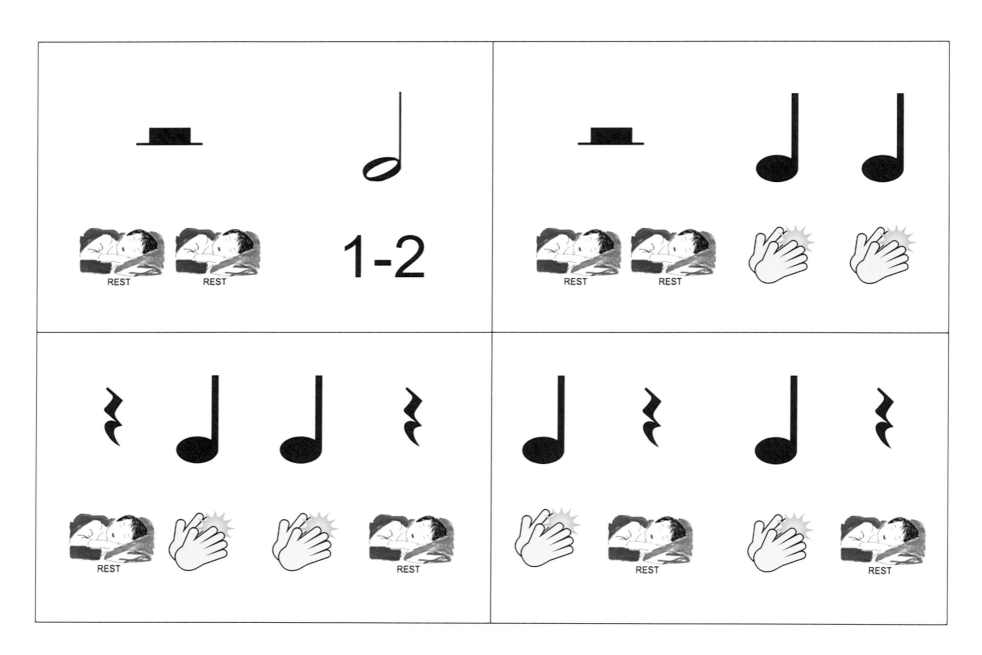

Figure 8.1l Rhythm exercise

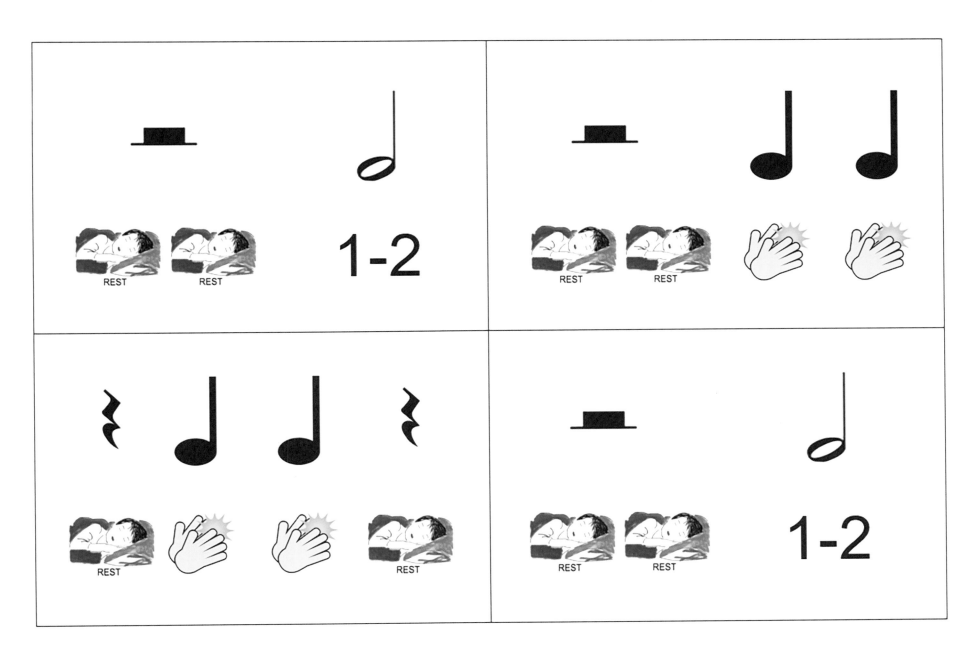

Figure 8.1m Rhythm exercise

8. Kinaesthesia and dyslexia

Another way I have found of resolving the problem of understanding notation values and rhythm is by encouraging my students to play the rhythm tree game. This uses large notes covered in felt or an equally tactile material. Figure 8.2 shows examples of the notes I have created, to include 1 whole note, 2 half notes, 4 quarter notes, 8 eighth notes, 16 sixteenth notes, 4 quarter note rests, 4 half note rests, 4 dots and the bass and treble clefs.

I give each note to my student, one by one, and I ask them to have a good look at each note and then feel its shape and direction. This engages both their visual and kinaesthetic senses. After they have looked at and felt each note, I tell them what the value of that note is. I then mix them up, pull out a note and ask my student for the note value. I use the American way of counting music. I have found my students remember the value of the notes by reference to their numerical worth more easily than by their name. However, this is a matter of personal choice. We play a quick game every week to see how many of the note values they have remembered. As an incentive, if they remember a minimum of 6, they can choose something from my treat box.

Figure 8.2 Felt notes

I then begin the process of creating a rhythm tree. The first time I create the tree I explain how the value of the notes relate to each other (i.e. 1 whole note (4) = 2 half notes (2+2)). Dependent upon the severity of the dyslexia, I may initially only put out the whole and half notes.

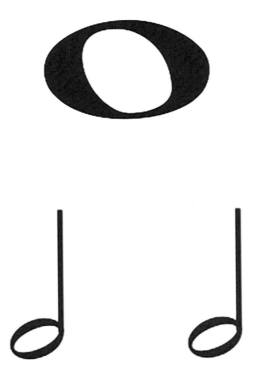

Figure 8.3a Rhythm tree exercise

When I am sure that my student understands how the value of the whole and half notes relate to each other, then I add the next layer of the rhythm tree (the quarter notes).

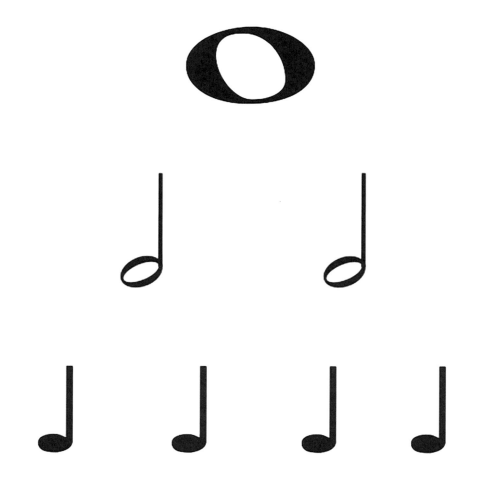

Figure 8.3b Rhythm tree exercise

Once I am sure that my student has understood how the value of the quarter notes relates to the whole notes and the half notes, I add the eighths and then the sixteenths.

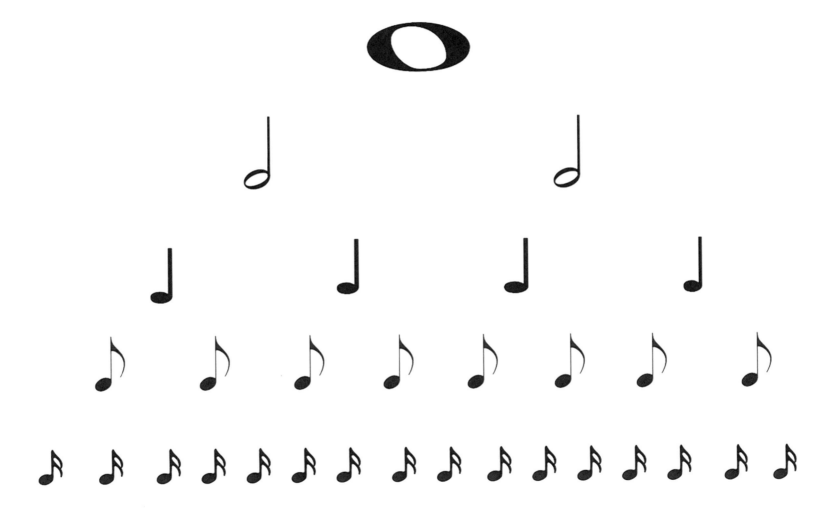

Figure 8.3c Rhythm tree exercise

When I am confident that my student understands how the note values relate to each other, I remove several notes. I then ask my students to fill in the gaps using identical missing notes. As they find each corresponding note, I ask them what the note is called. If they give the wrong note name, I encourage them to try again. If they cannot remember I will tell them. How regularly we do this depends upon the student.

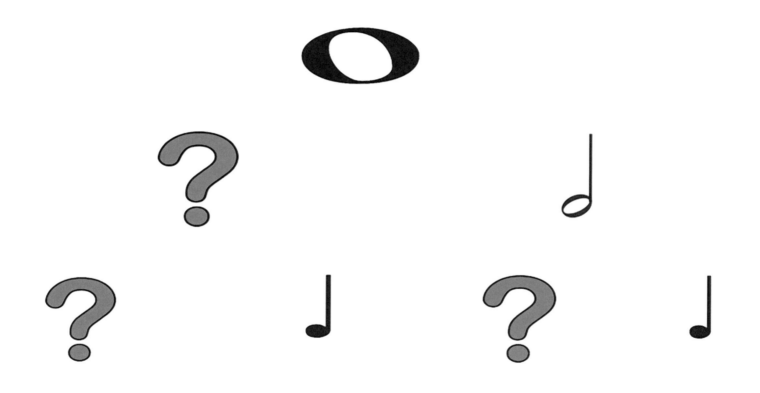

Figure 8.3d Rhythm tree exercise

Once a student is confident with adding the identical note, its notation value, and the direction it should be placed in, I once again remove several notes. I explain to my student that I need the gaps filled. This time they cannot use the identical note/s, instead they need to use alternative notes which add up to the same value as the missing note.

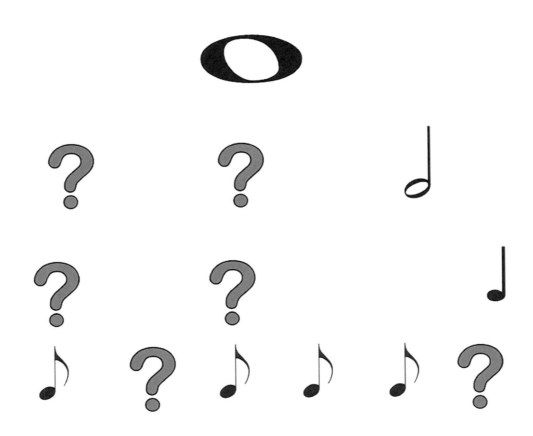

Figure 8.3e Rhythm tree exercise

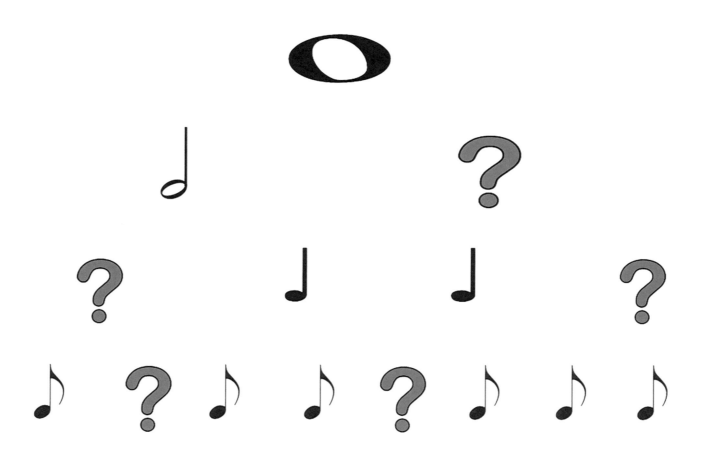

Figure 8.3f Rhythm tree exercise

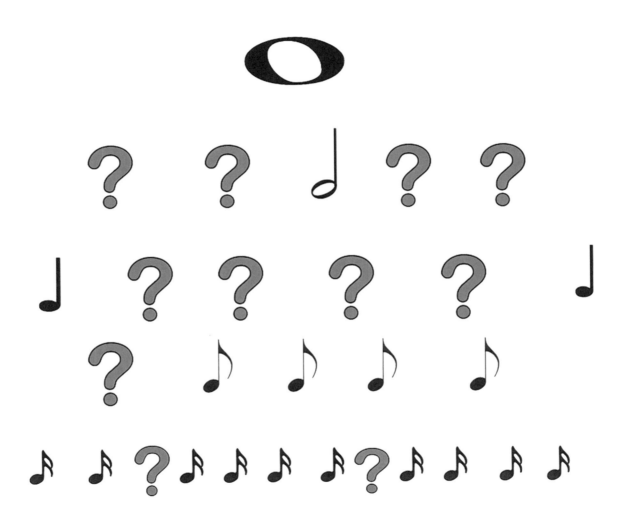

Figure 8.3g Rhythm tree exercise

8. Kinaesthesia and dyslexia

Time and time again I have seen an improvement in my students' sight-reading of note valuations and rhythm as we have played this game.

RHYTHM CLAPPING GAME

I also play the rhythm clapping game with my students. For example, I will ask them to begin clapping a steady 4/4 quarter beat while I clap out a 2/4 whole beat. I then get them to swap after about 20 seconds. There are numerous combinations of this game. You can clap out 4 quarter notes to 1 whole note, 2 half notes to their whole note, and so on. The one my students love most is their 2 eighth notes to my 1 quarter note. I always end up laughing with them when they realise I have made a mistake (normally deliberately).

Over time, you can incorporate the dotted notes and so on. It can take a little time for a student to understand the rhythms and to remember the dotted notes but, with constant repetition of these drill practices and perseverance, they will get there, and it is such a joy when they do.

CHECKLIST

1. If a student has problems with rhythms, what methods can you use to help them improve?
2. Have you factored into your lesson 5–10 minutes of rhythm exercises?
3. Have you bought some black and white plasticine and asked them to create a mini-score?
4. Have you bought some air clay and asked your students to create and paint the notes?
5. Have you factored time into your lessons for any of the rhythm games?
6. Have you discussed with your student's parent/guardian the possibility of them engaging in rhythm games at home?

9. LACK OF FOCUS

It is accepted that some dyslexics can have problems concentrating and may lack focus. I have students who, from the moment the lessons start, really concentrate and, in contrast, I have students I have to work hard to engage because they are distracted by the simplest things.

If you have a very busy studio, with pictures on the wall, books lying around and many items on display, there will be many questions about 'What is that?', 'What is this?', 'What is that for?' and 'What is this for?'. It really helps if your studio is neat and uncluttered. The less there is to distract your student's attention the more focused they will be. I do have anatomy and physiology pictures of the vocal tract, spine and diaphragm, so, if questions are asked, I can link the answers back to the lesson taking place at the time. However, my studio does look over my garden and I now have a good idea of the names of all the flora and fauna out there!

If a student tries to jump ahead in a lesson, this is likely to be because they are having difficulty with that specific part of the lesson. One of my students had a tendency to rush along, especially if she was stuck.

On one occasion I stopped the lesson to discuss this tendency and her response was fascinating, 'I know what it is, but it is stuck at the back of my head and I can't get it to come forward.' She was an incredibly intelligent and articulate person and one of the most lateral thinking people I have ever come across. However, she made silly mistakes because of an absolute need to 'get it right'. When she didn't, she could become frustrated. I was constantly having to get her to slow down and reassure her that she could take time to think it through. I found that the best solution was to take a step back from the exercise and switch to another exercise that I knew she could do easily. This helped her to refocus. I then returned to the more difficult exercise, first making sure that I had prepared her for the difficulties she might face.

In my experience, if the problem a student is having with visual stress and/or phonological processing is being addressed, then a student's lack of focus is much less evident.

Communication is key. In most instances once I explain to my students exactly what we are trying to achieve, and the methodology that will be applied, they will work hard to reach that particular goal. The work ethic of my dyslexic students is inspiring. They want to learn, they want to get it right, which is just one of the many reasons I love teaching them.

It is necessary to be flexible when teaching dyslexic students and these are just some of the methods I employ:

1. Even if I am working on theory or aurals, I start the lesson with breathing exercises, which help to create calmness

2. For students aged 11 and above I may reduce the lessons to around 40 minutes. As the student and I work together to explore the best multi-sensory teaching methods for their needs, they become engaged in the process. Before we know it, we are working beyond that 40 minutes. I then adjust the lesson time to 1 hour.

3. I ensure that the lesson is varied. Throughout the process I discuss and explain every aspect of what I am doing, and why I am giving an instruction. Of course, I do this with all my students, but with my dyslexic students I tend to be even more detailed.

4. I have pictures in my studios of the larynx, vocal cords and so on. Then, if students are distracted during the lesson and ask questions, it is more likely to be about something that I can use as a teaching aid.

5. I have a very large mirror in my studio. As we work together, I constantly remind them to copy my mouth/jaw/tongue position and encourage them to monitor what they are doing by checking their reflection. This helps to keep them focused.

CHECKLIST

1. Have you tidied your studio?
2. Have you considered commencing lessons with relaxing breathing exercises?
3. Have you considered initially providing shorter lessons?
4. Have you noticed if your student is trying to avoid a certain section of a lesson?
5. Are you varying your lessons?
6. Do you have a mirror in your studio, and is your student using it to check their posture and mouth/jaw/tongue position?

Because it is so important to employ a multi-sensory approach, there is quite a lot of physicality in my lessons, including:

(a) concentrating on breathing at the commencement of lessons. This has the double effect of helping students understand the correct method of breathing during songs and assisting them to become calm prior to working on technique, aurals and so on

(b) playing rhythm games that include clapping and jumping. I use physical exercises to help students understand various aspects of the music. I use stairs/steps to help students understand intervals. If we are working on major seconds, they stretch their leg to the 2nd step and for major third to the 3rd step, and so on. Admittedly, we normally only manage to get to a perfect 4th with this method, but you get the idea. If I am in a studio with a lot of space, we walk the music around the room. I mark out the length of the notes with black sewing tape as follows:

Eighth ___ quarter _____ half _____ whole _____ and my students then have to walk the notes.

So, for example they might have the following 4 bars of music to follow in 3/4 time:

— — —————

———— — ———

——————— ——

— — — —— — —

(c) when teaching sharps and flats I use the rabbit exercise:

Figure 10.1 Rabbit exercise

First, we read through a section of the music we are learning that contains sharps/flats and we note where all the sharps and flats are. Do not attempt more than 4 bars of music at one time. We then listen to the music and I ask them to imagine that they are a rabbit going for a walk by a field in the rhythm of the music (they can walk on the spot if space is limited). Every time they see/hear the sharp, they quickly go on tiptoe (in rhythm) to look over the fence at the carrots in the field, their rabbit ears pricked up as high as possible. Every time they see/hear the flat, their bodies slump, and their ears flatten because they have eaten so many carrots. I know it sounds silly, but I have tested it out and it works.

I keep small pictures of the rabbit drawings in a box and when my students see a sharp or flat they can place the correct rabbit over the correct accidental note as a little reminder.

(d) I use physicality and imagery to help students who have difficulty remembering Italian/German dynamic markings (see Figures 10-1a–e):

Allegro: we sit on the floor and bring our legs up to our chests and extend them quickly (to grow). This physical action acts as a reminder when they see the word but cannot remember either how to pronounce it or what it means – it also means you laugh a lot with your student.

Figure 10.2a Allegro multi-sensory

Allegretto: I place a piece of grey cloth over the student's foot and then we look at our legs and say the word sadly.

AH LEG GREY TOE

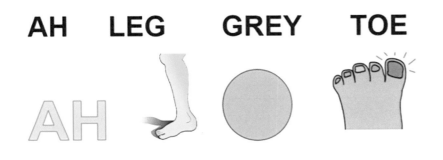

Figure 10.2b Allegretto multi-sensory

Staccato: we make a star with our arms, then pretend to drive our car and then touch our toe.

STAR CAR TOE

Figure 10.2c Staccato multi-sensory

Arpeggio: we make a disgusted face and say 'Ahr', imagine putting a peg on our nose (to stop a smell) and then, because of the smell, we go, but you have to remember to break down the word go into its separate letters, G and O.

AR PEG GI O

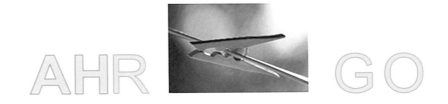

Figure 10.2d Arpeggio multi-sensory

Canto: I get my student to hit a tin can with their toe, as though it was a football.

CAN TOE

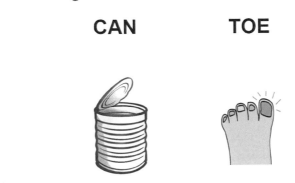

Figure 10.2e Canto multi-sensory

Legato: my student and I look at our leg in wonder and then loudly say AH as we discover our toe.

LEG   AH   TOE

Figure 10.2f Legato multi-sensory

Piano and Forte: we make ourselves as small as possible and I get my students to whisper pppppppppppppppppppp and then to spread their arms and reach for the sky and shout forte (with children we jump up, with youths and adults we stretch up).

Once I have told a student what a musical term means, I get them to tell me what imagery comes to their mind that will help them to remember that term. We then use **their** imagery to recall it.

(e) To help students understand how a music scores fits together I ask them to complete music jigsaws for me. I photocopy a song and then cut it up so that the components are separated. I ask them to reassemble the score by putting the various pieces back in order.

Figure 10.3 Music jigsaw

I constantly apply multi-sensory techniques throughout the teaching process until I find the combination that works most effectively for that student. The combination of aids and methods will differ with each one.

CHECKLIST

1. Are you using physical exercises to assist your student to learn kinaesthetically?
2. Are you exploring different combinations of multi-sensory exercises?
3. Have you asked your student for their ideas about creating visual images and physical movements to remember music terms?

11. COPING WITH VISUAL STRESS AND PHONOLOGICAL METHODS WITH DEEP DYSLEXIA

I have students who have severe forms of dyslexia. This makes them anxious and affects their self-esteem. They tend to be very, very hardworking and very, very self-critical.

At the beginning of this book you may remember I said I was determined that no other student would ever have a negative experience during a singing lesson with me again. That I would find a way of teaching students with learning disabilities, no matter how severe the disability. This has made me test various methods to find the most effective methods for teaching students impacted by deep dyslexia.

One of the first things I learnt was that if you present a student with deep dyslexia with a full music score they will become anxious, even if it is upsized and on appropriately coloured paper. Each adjustment to enhance visual stress will help build confidence. However, issues with difficulties in phonological processing can swiftly undermine the progress made.

It has therefore been necessary for me to think laterally. The question I have had to ask myself is, 'How can I teach music theory and practice to cause as little anxiety as possible and to empower my students?'

When talking to one of my students it became clear that they loved football. It occurred to me that this was a sport with a structure. So I read up on formations in football and came across the 4-4-2 formation. I immediately thought of my rhythm trees. Next time I saw my student I decided to test out my theory.

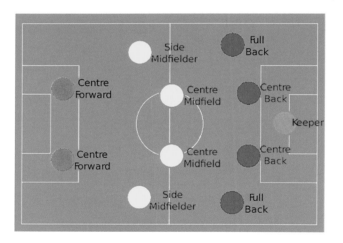

Figure 11.1 Football

I explained that the goalie was a whole note, the centre forwards were the half notes, and the fullbacks,

112

centre backs, side midfielders and centre midfielders were the quarter notes. At the same time I showed him a picture of a rhythm tree.

The first thing I noticed was that my student became more relaxed as we talked about the similarities between the rhythm tree and the picture of the 4-4-2 formation. I could see that he had made the connection between structure and formation in football and structure and formation in music. He commented, 'That helps me understand better.'

Whenever I can, I look for an activity that my student loves and, if I can find any link to rhythm or notation values, I try to apply that connection in a way that assists my student in the learning process. It does not always work, but I have had over a 50% success rate so far.

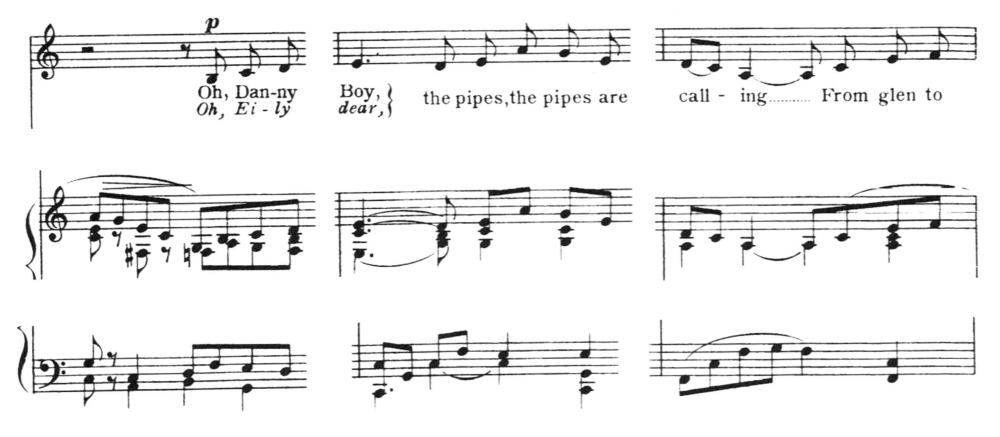

Figure 11.2 Danny Boy

Sometimes, due to the severity of the impact of dyslexia on my student, it has been necessary for me to break the music down almost bar by bar. At this stage it is not that they cannot see the music clearly (hopefully, we have improved issues with visual stress using the methods above), rather, it is the sheer amount of information they are having to deal with from the music score. This overwhelms them as they struggle with the phonological processing issues.

As I am predominantly a singing and theory teacher, the first thing I do is break the music down bar by bar to separate out the melody line, the first harmonic line and the second harmonic line. See the example of *Oh Danny Boy* in Figure 11.2

It is time-consuming, but it needs to be done slowly to build up a student's confidence. My method of teaching a student with this level of severe dyslexia is specific (but I am sure you can make adaptations that work just as effectively).

At the beginning of the process of learning a song, I sing the first phrase to them and they then repeat it back to me. I make sure that the music I start them off with has a very defined pattern and structure within it. I repeat this call and response pattern until they have learnt the first phrase of the song and are confident.

Then I introduce one bar of music and ask them if they can see any sort of pattern. Are the notes going up like steps? Are they coming down like steps? Are they all on the same line? Are they the same note values? What do the note values add up to?

Then together we physicalise the notes. For *Danny Boy* I raise my hand four times consecutively, in steps for the first four notes, and then get them to sing that section of the song looking at the notes and using their hand to rise and fall with the notes.

the pipes,the pipes are

Figure 11.3a Danny Boy

When my student is confident with the first bar of the melody and can tell me if there are any dynamic markings in that bar of music, I add the second bar of music. We learn this and then add the two bars together until the first phrase of the song is learnt. Obviously, we are constantly revisiting the previous bars of music that have already been learnt. This assists with the repetition, drill and practice work.

If it is clear that we are not going to be able to learn the whole of the first phrase, I just concentrate on two bars of music and set the next two bars as homework. Once they have mastered the melody line of the first phrase, we may take a small break if we manage to achieve this within one lesson.

I then explain how important it is to know what is happening in the left hand. That it is in the left hand that the composer of the music provides us with information about how he wants the song/music performed. I tell them that I am going to add the harmonic accompaniment. In this way, I am not only breaking down the music physically, I am also breaking down my explanation. This provides my dyslexic student with time to process the information I am imparting.

I repeat that music is made up of patterns, and that we need to find the patterns in the music. I ask them if they can find a pattern in the music in the first harmonic line that matches anything in the melody line. I do show them the first pattern and then ask them to find the next pattern. When they get it, I tend to get very excited and I say something like, 'I thought you told me you had a problem with the music? Well, maybe it is not as much of a problem as you thought it was.'

I then get them to find the next pattern. This can be a slow process, but watching their realisation that there is a structure and a method that they can follow, fills me with such joy and excitement. As I type this, I am getting that feeling and I wish I could share with you the level of pleasure I feel in their achievement.

I then give them homework – the second musical phrase, broken down bar by bar into the melody and first harmonic line (numbered). I ask them to go through the music, find the patterns, mark them up with a highlighter and then to Sellotape the music together.

During this process we discuss and explore how you might have a minim in the first harmonic line, but two crochets in the melody. And I help them learn to count the music, which is a bit of a bugbear with me. Counting the music is another way of providing structure for the dyslexic student. I have found that my dyslexic students like structure, structure is dependable.

I also begin to point out that there is a pattern downwards (chords) as well as across the music. Each student is individual, so I have to assess when I can put this concept to them. Once I feel confident that they understand that there are two patterns in the music, one across and one downwards, I then add the second harmonic line.

Figures 11.3b–c Danny Boy

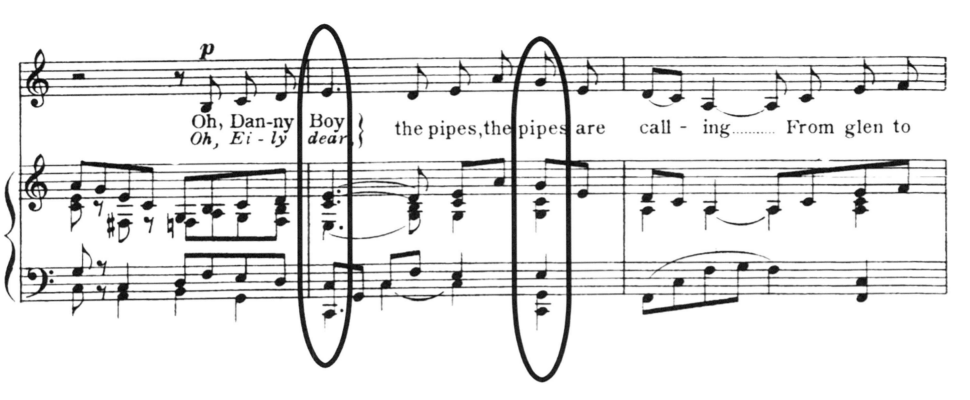

Figure 11.3d Danny Boy

Again, I cut the music up, bar by bar, and I ask them to mark up the chords.

During each of these stages my student is only concentrating on one small section of the score, which is far less overwhelming than being faced with the full score.

I establish with them where the chords are in the first phrase of the song (I never present my student with more than 4 bars of music at this stage of proceedings). I ask them to go through the first phrase of music and to mark out each and every chord. I will not spend a whole lesson doing this but just start them off with this task. I establish in the lesson that they can see the score clearly and understand what I want them to do and then ask them to finish the task at home. I also provide 2 bars of a totally new song. I mark out the first chord and then ask them to complete this as well. If they do not return the work even partially attempted, it is in an indicator that they have not totally understood what I have said, so I go through all the information again, but even more slowly than previously. I also monitor myself very carefully to make sure that there can be no confusion about the instructions I am giving. I scan and send them the music to view on their computers/ laptops as sometimes it helps my students to see the score more easily.

CHECKLIST

1. Can you ascertain whether your student has a hobby that they love? Is there anything in that hobby that you could use as a link to assist them in learning about rhythm or notation values?
2. Have you begun to learn the song/instrumental music vocally, using the echo method?
3. Have you broken up the song/instrumental music into bars and then separated out the harmonic lines?
4. Are you learning the melody bar by bar and then adding the bars together as your student learns the relationship between the words and the notation?
5. Have you considered adding the first harmonic line and encouraging your student to discover the patterns in the music?
6. Have you considered, when would be the best time to add the second harmonic line to the music and how to assist your student to learn the chords?

12. ASSISTIVE TECHNOLOGY FOR EXAM PREPARATIONS

The positive impact of assistive technology is being acknowledged for the support it can give the dyslexic student. It therefore seemed totally logical to me that this technology could be used to assist my students. I investigated Musescore, a free notation software program, and began experimenting to see what aid it could offer my students. I found that many of the adjustments referred to above could be achieved using this program. I took some old ABRSM exam papers and incorporated the exercises into some music scores I created on Musescore. I then trained my students to:

- Access and set up Musescore
- Access the revision exercises I had prepared for them on Musescore.

My students' responses to being taught using assistive technology was a revelation. One had no issues with visual stress, but she did have considerable problems with phonological processing, in particular with memory retrieval. We had an extended lesson of 1.5 hours when I trained her on how to use Musescore. I could see that she really enjoyed the process, and I could also see that she was really enjoying the training. I was then unable to see her for two weeks. When I arrived for our next lesson a fortnight later, I presumed that we would have to start all over again. We started the process of opening a new music score in Musescore and I watched in wonder and excitement as she opened the score, requiring limited assistance from me. She was hesitant at times, but I only had to begin to tell her what to do and she would just run ahead of me – and she was loving the process. I came away from that lesson buzzing with excitement.

But my greatest joy was the response of a student with a severe form of dyslexia. Not only did she have difficulty with visual processing, but she also had difficulty with phonological processing. She would become anxious and frustrated easily if I did not break down the work into small units. I trained her on how to open Musescore and we viewed it on a large 65 inch screen. Again, I watched in wonder at the speed with which she absorbed instructions to open and set up the program. Once I had completed the training, I asked her to set up a music score on her own. She remembered virtually every aspect of the training immediately. Within a very short time she was finding shortcuts I didn't know existed. I showed her how to access the theory exercises I had prepared, which required her to add bar lines, fill in notes in chords, create stated intervals and so on. After she started the exercises, she just got on with completing the tasks, and she required hardly any assistance. I then began sending her exercises to complete at home, which she managed without me, getting the majority of them right.

I decided to take it a stage further and asked her to compose a piece of music. I taught her how to compose using a simple C major chord. I wish I could show you her composition, but since I gave her a very strong lecture on copyright issues, I am unable to do so. I was so impressed with the standard of the final composition that I had to ask her if she had completed it on her own. Other than a little assistance in respect of repeated patterns, she had not received any help. I noted that when she worked in this manner her anxiety levels dropped completely and her comment about using assistive technology was, 'It's cool.'

As a matter of course, I now use assistive technology as yet another aid when teaching my dyslexic students. This is always mixed with teaching on paper because, ultimately, the exams will be taken on paper. The confidence my students gain by using assistive technology translates into the work they need to do on paper, although they can find it more onerous.

When one of my dyslexic students is due to take their exams, I contact the appropriate exam body in advance and inform them of the reasonable adjustments that my student will need, these include:

- five minutes of extra examining time to be used as necessary, of which up to three minutes to study the sight-reading test
- use of the scale book or lyrics for reference purposes
- use of visual overlay sheets
- alternative arrangements for aural tests if required
- extra time in music theory exams
- upsized exam papers and sight-reading sheets
- coloured music scores.

For full details of:

ABRSM Access Arrangements and Reasonable Adjustments go to https://gb.abrsm.org/media/63977/access-policy-for-website.pdf

Trinity Exams Special Need's Policy go to https://www.trinitycollege.com/qualifications/music/special-needs

London College of Music's Special Need's Policy go to https://lcme.uwl.ac.uk/equality-of-opportunity-reasonable-adjustment-and-special-consideration

I have described many of the adjustments that are required when teaching the dyslexic student. Although I think it is necessary to ensure that students engage in the physical reading and writing of music on paper, I consider that assistive technology, namely, the notation software program Musescore is a useful aid. It can assist the dyslexic music student to acquire the skills and knowledge they need to complete their exams successfully and to a high standard. I have found it of great assistance when teaching my dyslexic students. It is free and therefore easily accessible to all students. I presume other music notation software programs, such as Sibelius and Noteworthy, have the same tools but I have not tried them.

DOWNLOAD AND INSTALL MUSESCORE

For Word go to https://musescore.org/en/handbook/install-windows

For Mac go to https://musescore.org/en/handbook/install-macos

For Chromebook go to https://musescore.org/en/handbook/install-chromebook

For Linux go to https://musescore.org/en/handbook/install-linux

Once a dyslexic student has downloaded Musescore, it can be viewed on a TV, projector, computer or laptop. Students can easily customise the inbuilt tools to include the majority of the assistive methods referred to in this book as follows:

- the background colour of the score sheet can be changed
- text can be enlarged
- text fonts can be changed
- text colour can be changed
- coloured notes and staves can be used
- bar lines can be added in a contrasting colour
- different coloured accidentals can be added
- notes can be named as they are inputted
- direction of music note stems can be changed easily.

The process of using the software requires the student to use visual, auditory and kinaesthetic modes. Further benefits of using Musescore are:

- it can be used in 66 different languages
- there are videos that show how Musescore works
- notes can be sounded as they are played
- it can be displayed on TV screens, which makes it easier for students to see.

Once you have opened Musescore you will need to adjust the size of the Palette. All computer systems are different so you may need to adjust my instructions so that they work with your computer, but once Musescore is installed the instructions on how to adapt the music scores should be applicable whether you are using Word, Mac, Chromebook or Linux.

Each computer allows the text size to be increased but you may not be aware that you can also use a magnifier on your computer, and this is necessary to upsize the Musescore Palette, which will help with the symptoms of visual stress. The instructions I give are for Word, but if you use different software you should be able to find corresponding settings on your computer. Please be aware that Musescore is constantly bringing out updated versions and the following instructions relate to Musescore 3.4.

HOW TO UPSIZE THE MUSESCORE PALETTE

Open up your screen and in the search button type in Magnifier.

Figure 12.1a Musescore: start

The magnifer box will appear at 100%.

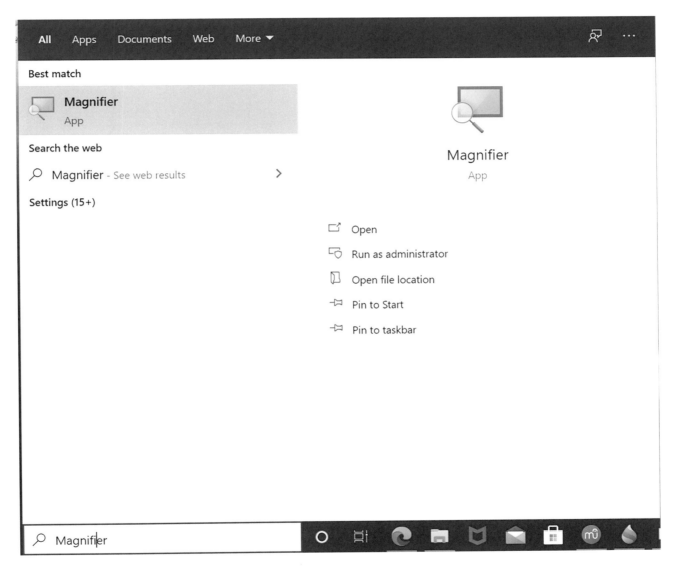

Figure 12.1b Musescore magnifier

12. Assistive technology

You can adjust the view from 200% to 800%. At 200% everything on the screen is double its original size.

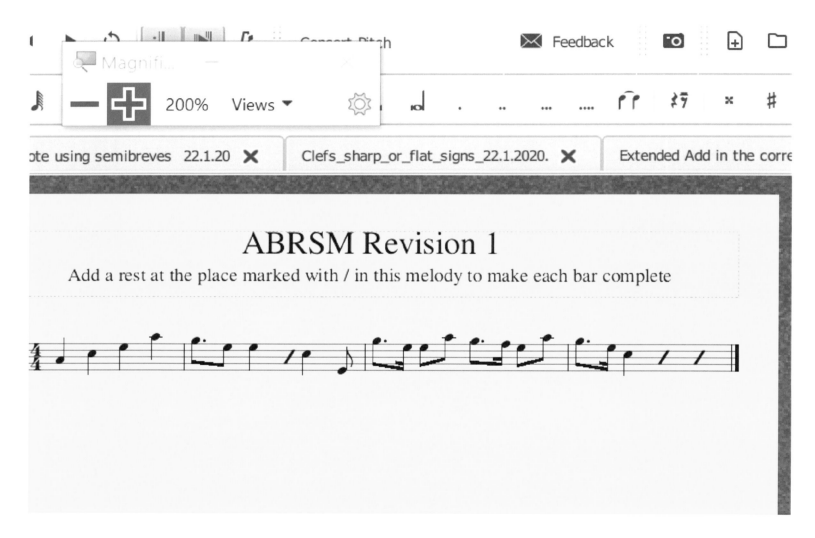

Figure 12.1c Musescore: magnifier at 200%

Alternatively, you can go to view and then zoom in to upsize. When you magnify the screen above 400% in Musescore the screen becomes difficult to view, you may prefer just to magnify the palette or a section of the screen.

In that case, click on View in the magnifier box and then on Lens.

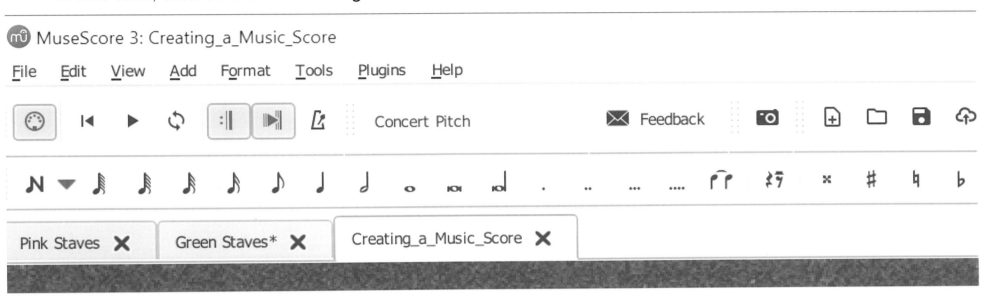

Figure 12.1d Musescore: using zoom and lens

A square lens will appear, place it over the section of the screen you want to see and increase it.

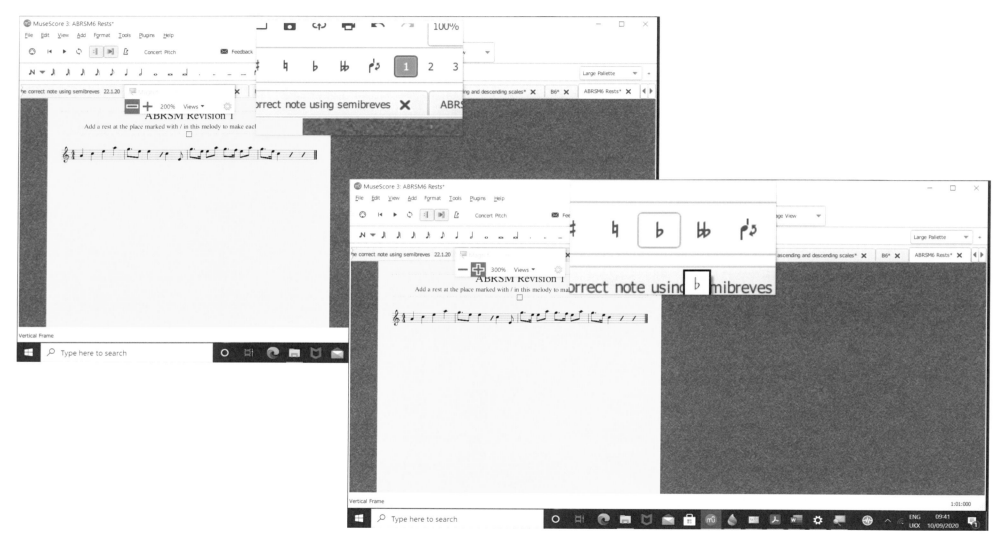

Figure 12.1e Musescore lens at 200% (top) and 300% (bottom)

I will now give you simple instructions for you and your students to set up your Musescore Score. I use a mixture of magnifying the palette and screen with the lens or I just increase the size of the screen.

To create a new music score, click on File, then Create New Score and the following window will appear.

Magnifi...

200% Views ▼   ⚙   Plugins   Help

🎵 New Score Wizard

Create New Score
    Enter score information:

Title:

Subtitle:

Composer:

Lyricist:

Figure 12.1f Musescore: create a new score

12. Assistive technology

Type in all the details: the name of your composition, your name and so on. Then hit next.

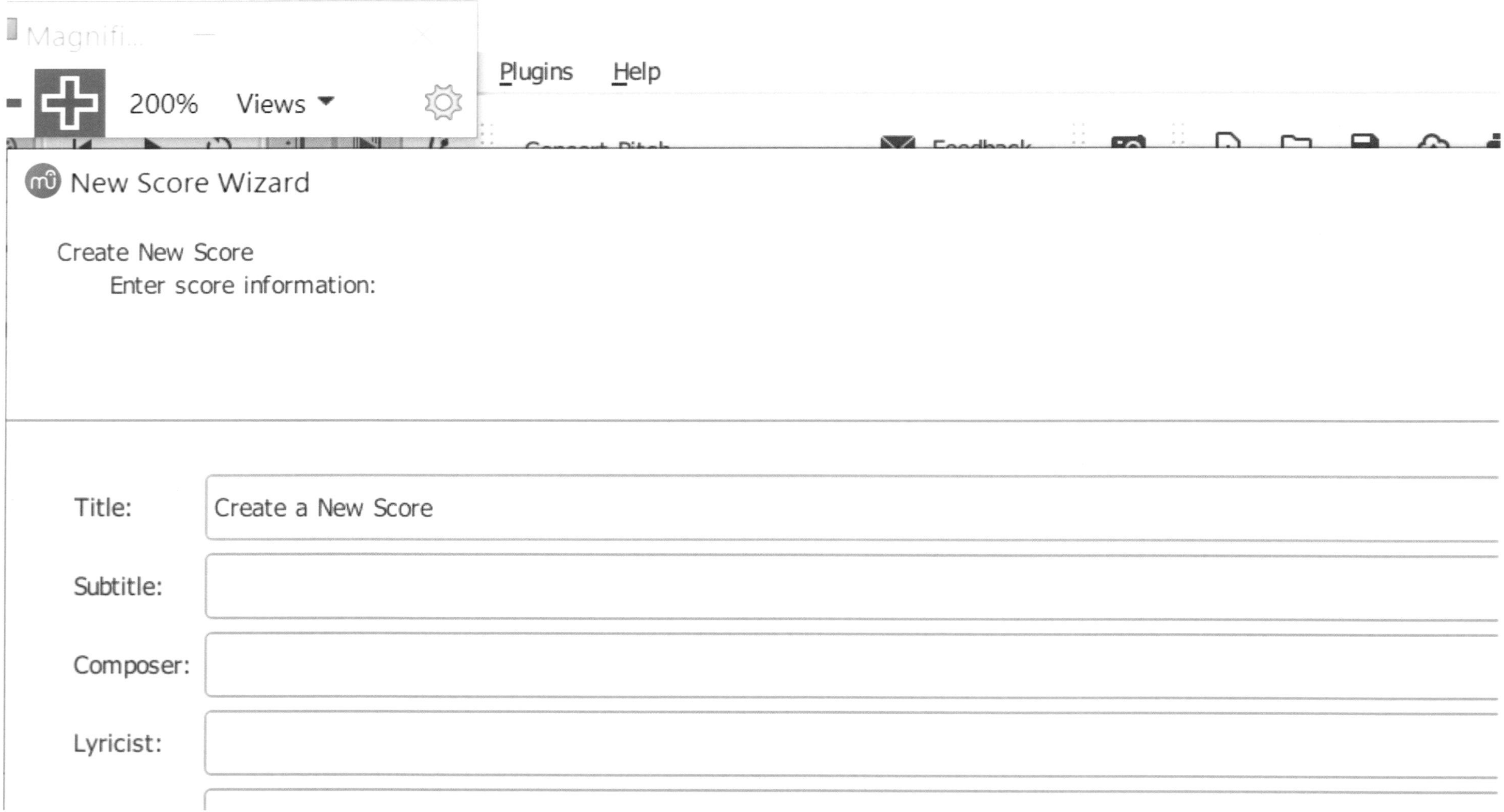

Magnifi...

200%   Views ▼

Plugins   Help

New Score Wizard

Create New Score
Enter score information:

Title: Create a New Score

Subtitle:

Composer:

Lyricist:

Figure 12.1g Musescore: details of new score

Choose the clef or instrument you want to compose with and click Next.

Figure 12.1h Musescore: setting up template

Choose which key you want to work in and click Next.

 New Score Wizard

Create New Score
    Choose key signature and tempo:

Key Signature

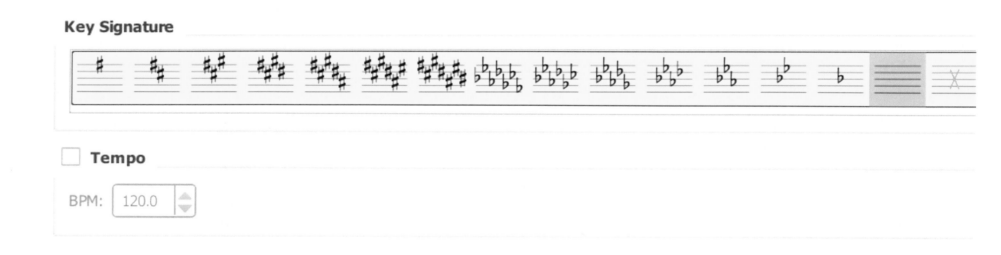

☐ **Tempo**

BPM: | 120.0 | ⬍

Figure 12.1i Musescore: choosing the key signature

Choose your time signature and click Next.

 New Score Wizard

Create New Score
    Choose time signature:

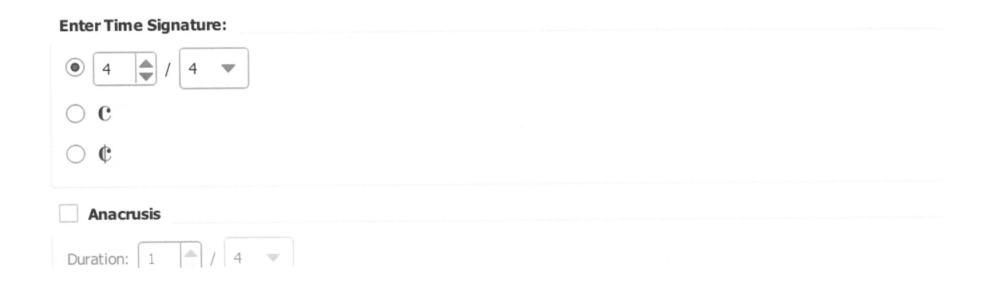

Figure 12.1j Musescore: choosing the time signature

          12. Assistive technology

A score will appear. To input the notes go to Add and then Notes.

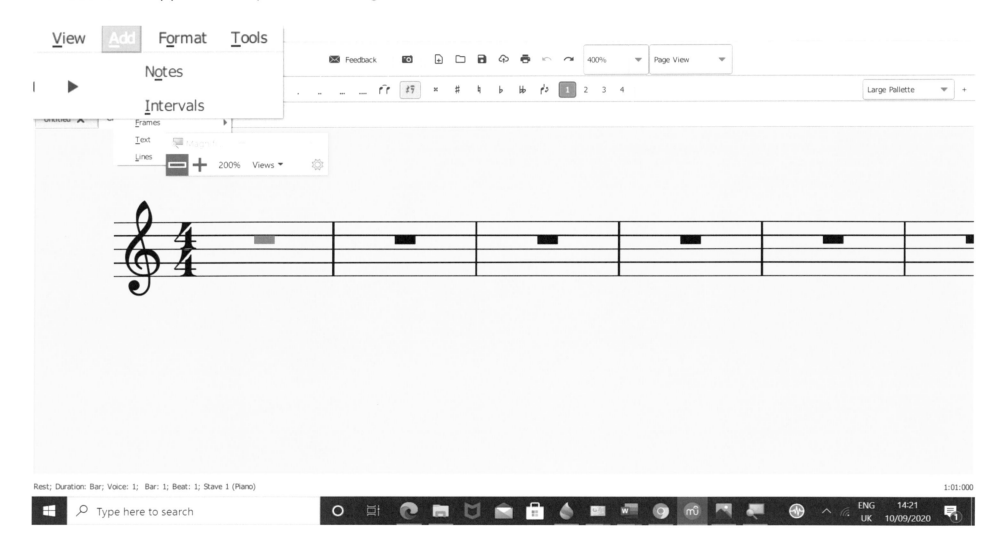

Figure 12.1k Musescore: adding notes

To start inputting the notes click on Add, then Notes, then put a tick in the Note Input box.
When you have finished inputting the notes remember to remove the tick.

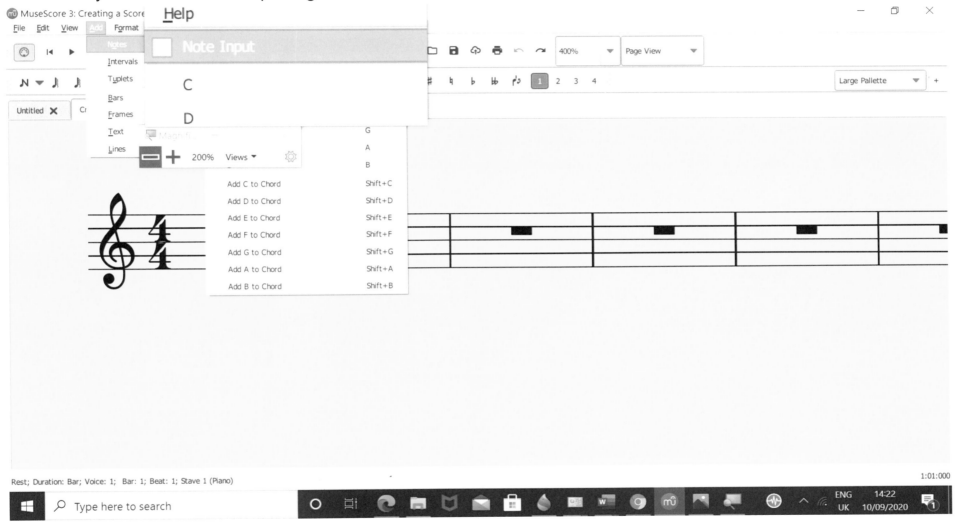

Figure 12.1l Musescore: note input

Choose the notes you want to use from the palette and place them where you want them to go on the blank score, each note will initially look blue.

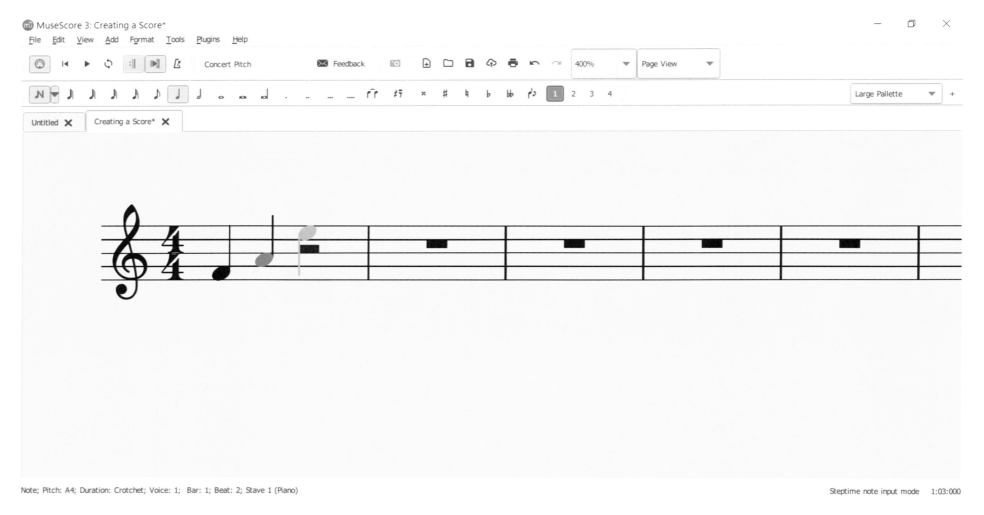

Figure 12.1m Musescore: inserting notes

As you can see, the notes eventually become black.

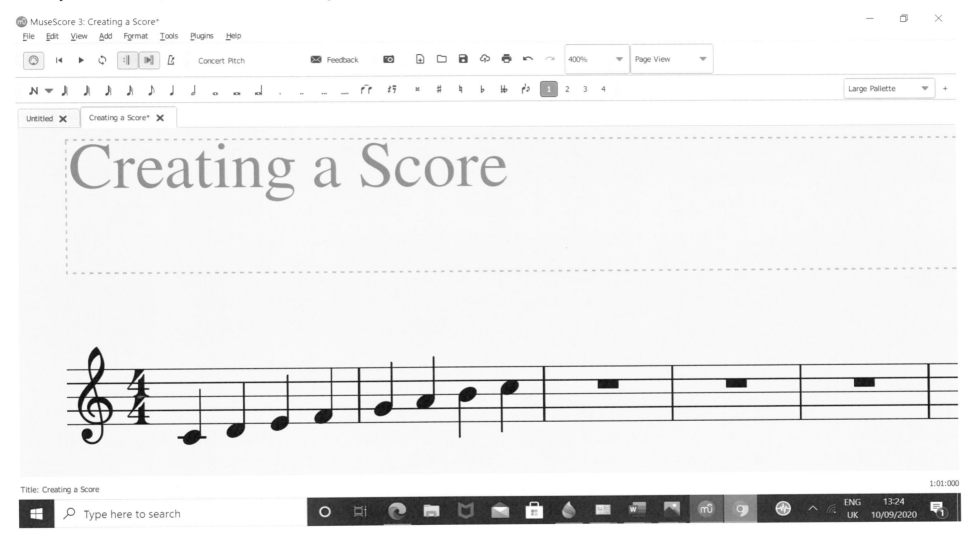

Figure 12.1n Musescore: note colour change

If you want to add the names of the notes, click on Plugins, Notes and then Note Names.

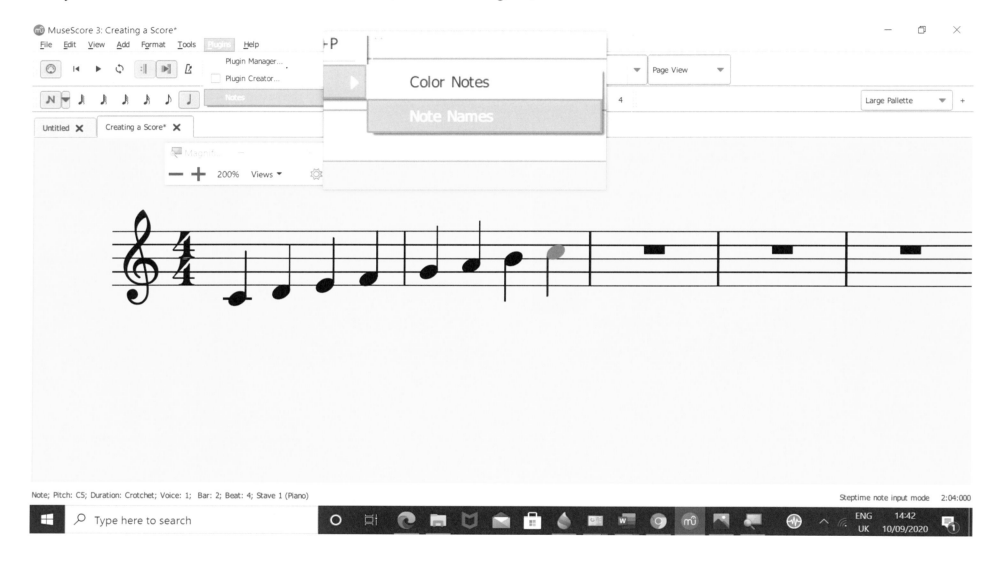

Figure 12.1o Musescore: plugin for naming notes

The names of the notes will appear.

Figure 12.1p Musescore: names on notes

To colour the notes go back to Plugin, click on Notes and then click on Color Notes.

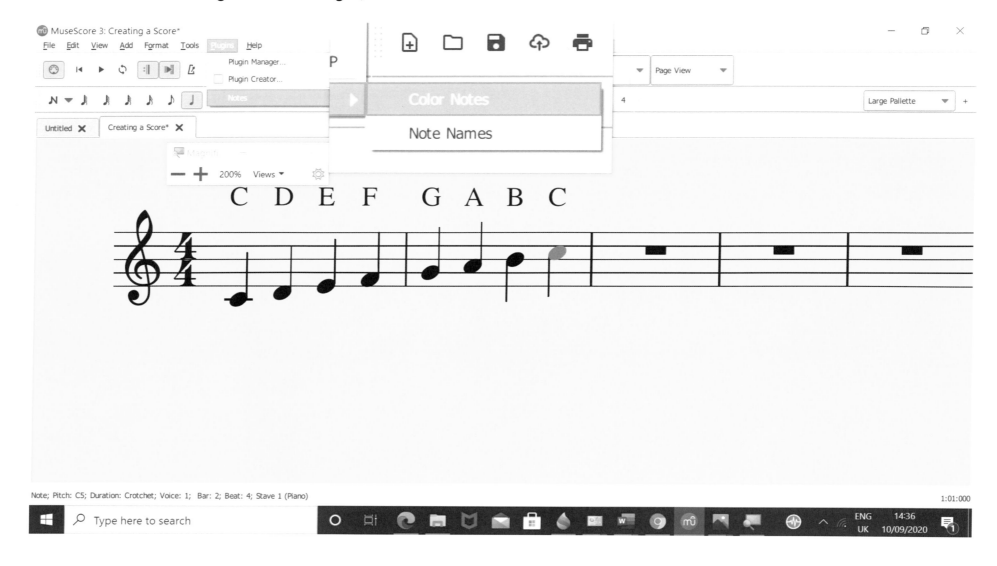

The notes will change colour.

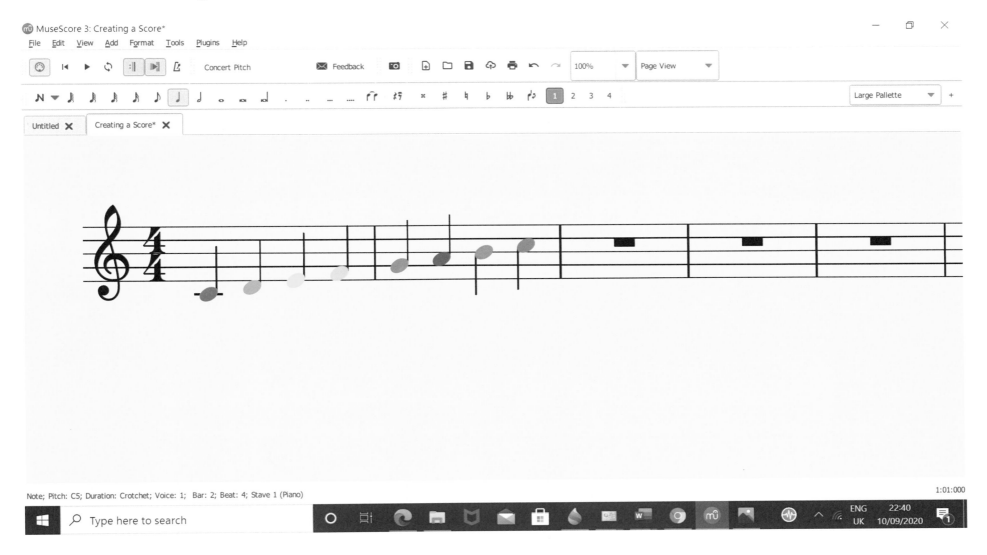

Figure 12.1r Musescore: coloured notes

12. Assistive technology

To add in your accidentals, highlight the note that you want to sharpen or flatten, then go to appropriate accidental and click on it. The accidental will immediately appear in front of the note.

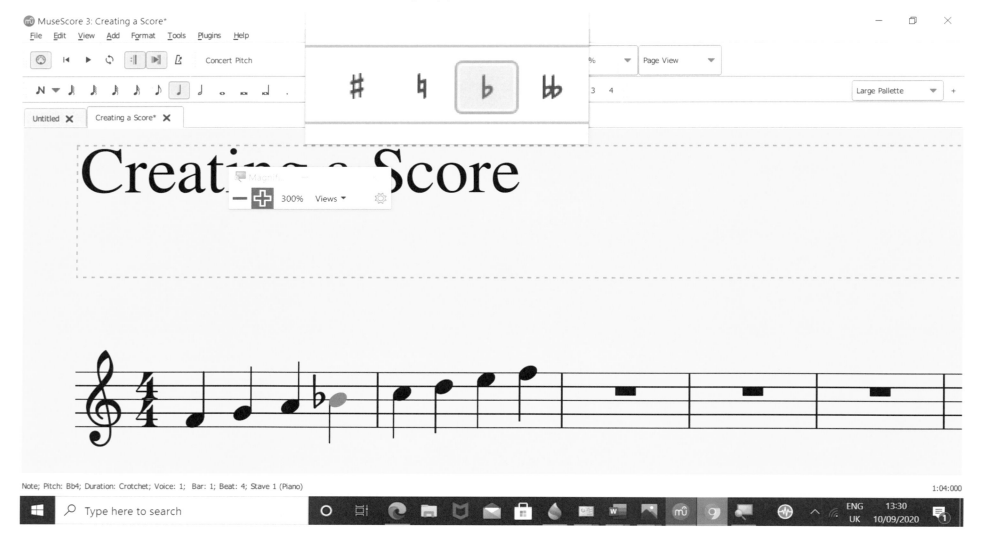

Figure 12.1s Musescore: adding accidentals

Note that if you are working with coloured notes the accidental will appear in the same colour as the note it is attached to.

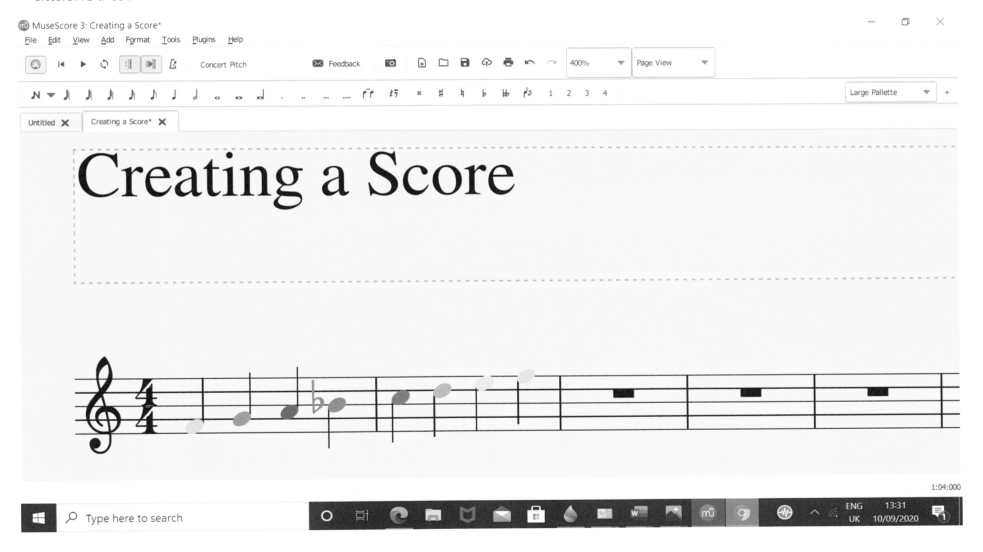

Figure 12.1t Musescore: coloured accidentals

12. Assistive technology

To change the score's background colour, click on Edit and then Preferences.

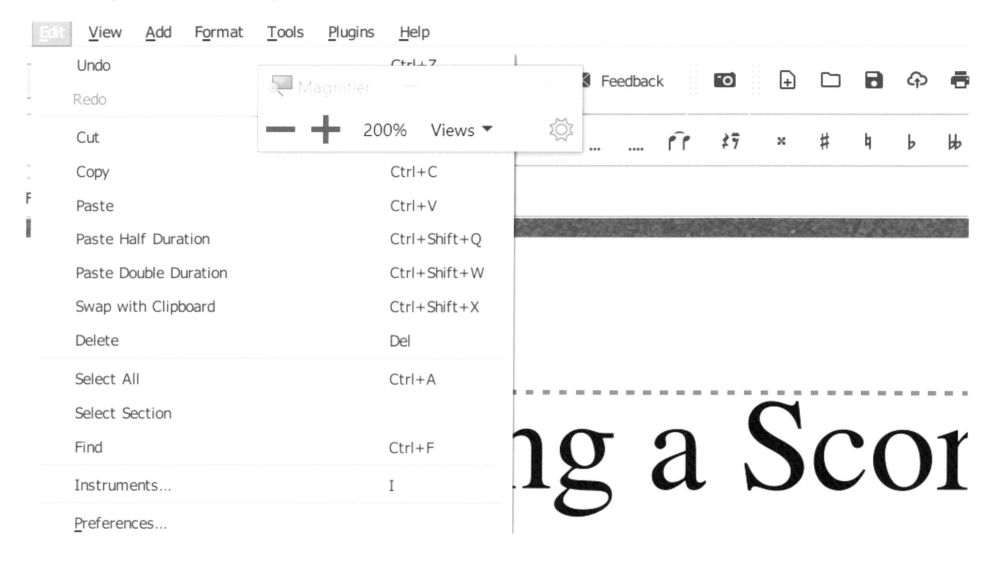

Figure 12.1u Musescore: changing background colour

Then click on Canvas. Go to the colour bar under Paper and click on the colour that is already present (in this picture it is yellow).

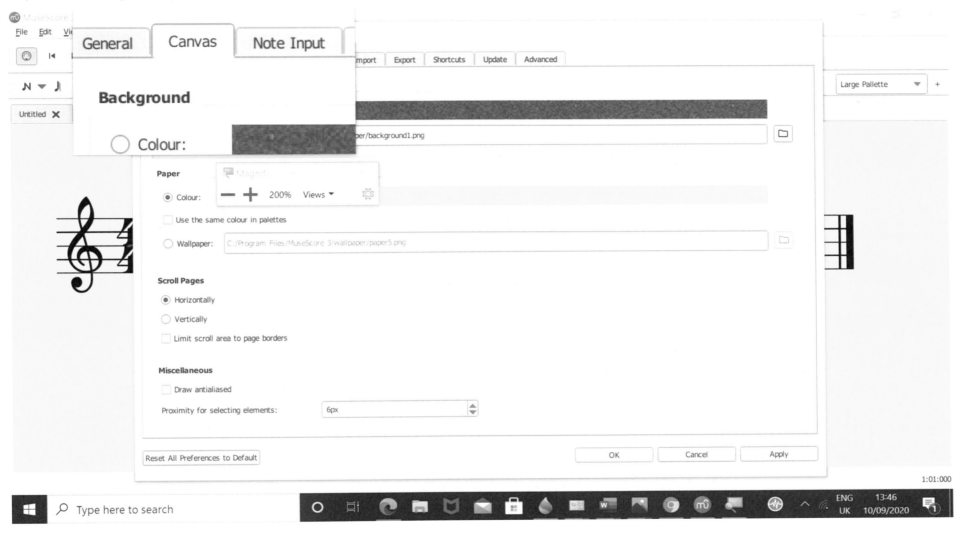

Figure 12.1v Musescore: background colour preferences

A palette box of colours appears. In this picture, I have clicked on a pale blue.

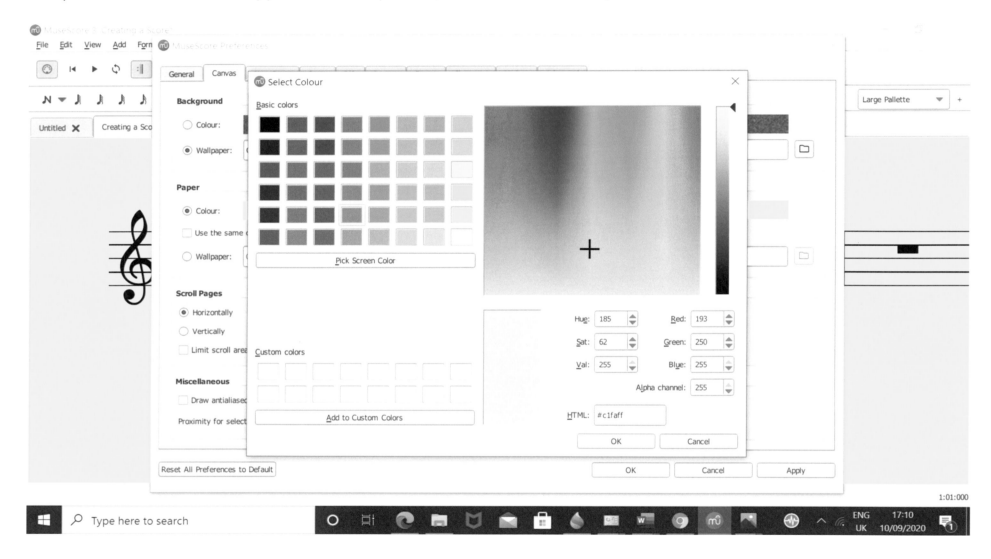

Figure 12.1w Musescore: choosing background colour

Once you are happy with the colour, click on OK and the background colour will change.

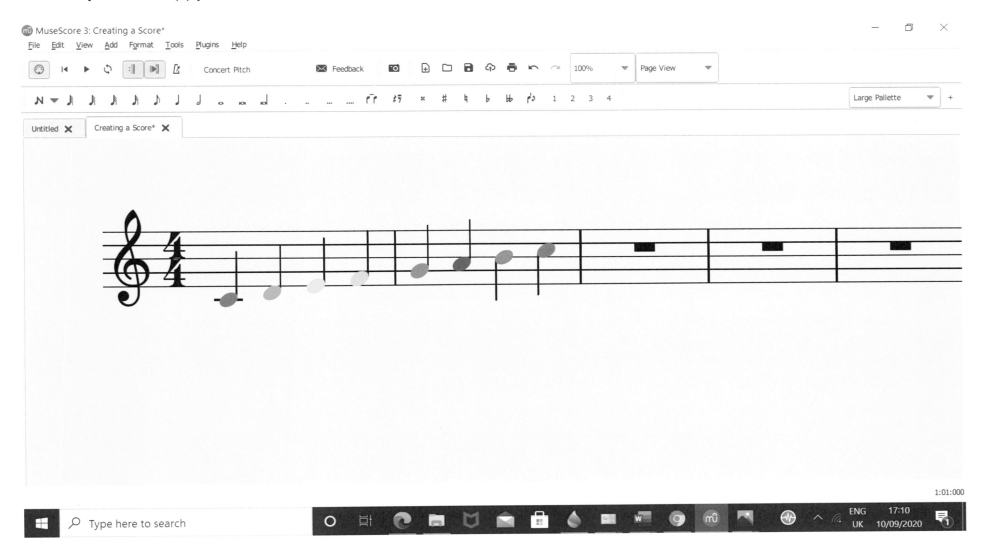

Figure 12.1x Musescore: new background colour

If you want to change the colour of the clef or the key signature, in fact of any component on the score, you need to highlight it (in the picture I have highlighted the treble clef), then click on View and then on Inspector.

Figure 12.1y Musescore: changing component colours, first step

A grey box will appear. Click on the black bar that is in the grey box.

Figure 12.1z Musescore: changing component colours, second step

Once again, the colour palette will appear. In this picture I clicked on red.

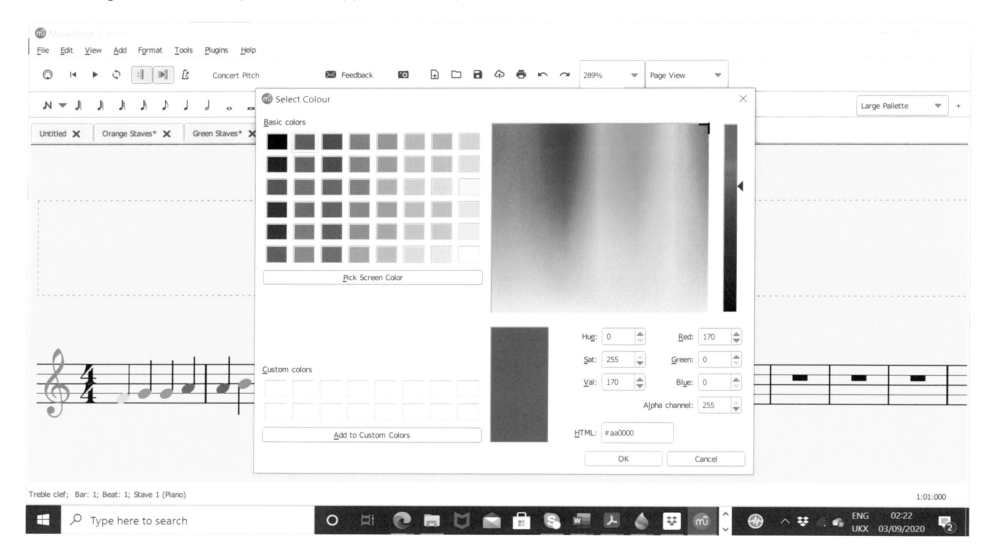

Figure 12.1aa Musescore: changing component colours. third step

As you can see, the treble clef has changed from black to red.

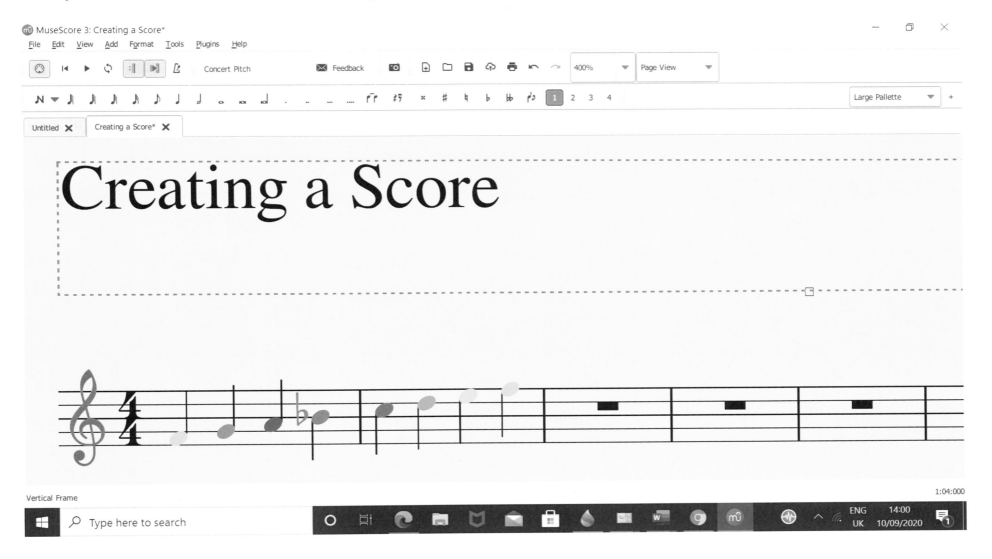

Figure 12.1bb Musescore: changed colour of treble clef

This picture shows that I have changed the colour of the time signature to blue, using exactly the same steps.

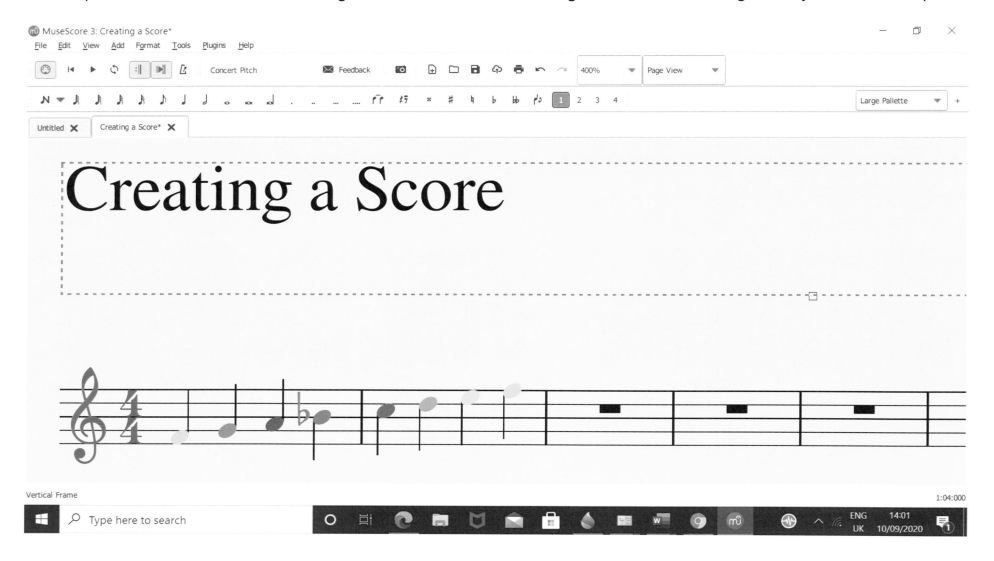

Figure 12.1cc Musescore: changed colour of time signature

To remove empty bars, highlight the bars you want to remove and click on Tools. A list will appear, scroll down to Remove Empty Trailing Bars and click on it. The empty bars will instantly disappear.

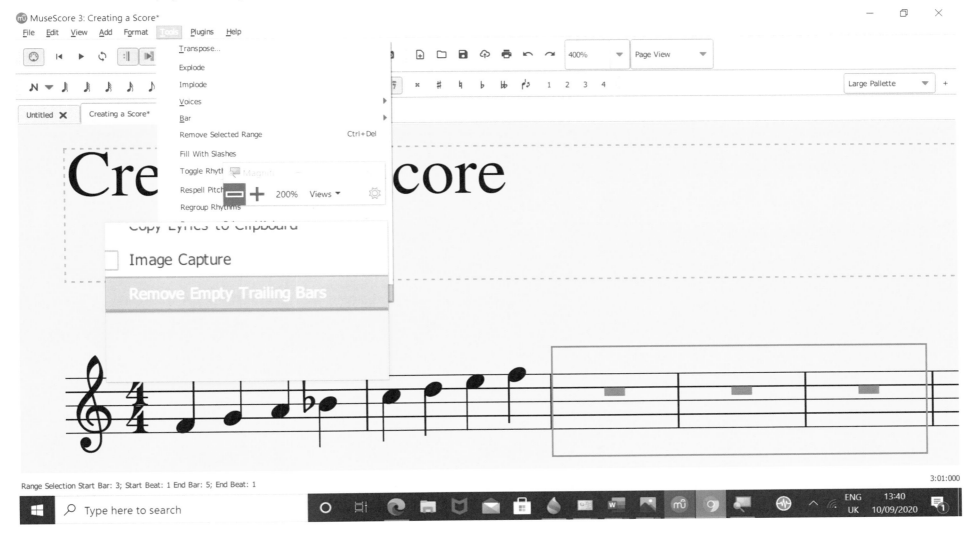

Figure 12.1dd Musescore: remove empty trailing bars

12. Assistive technology

To add bars, go to Add. Click on Bars, choose the option you want and follow the instructions.

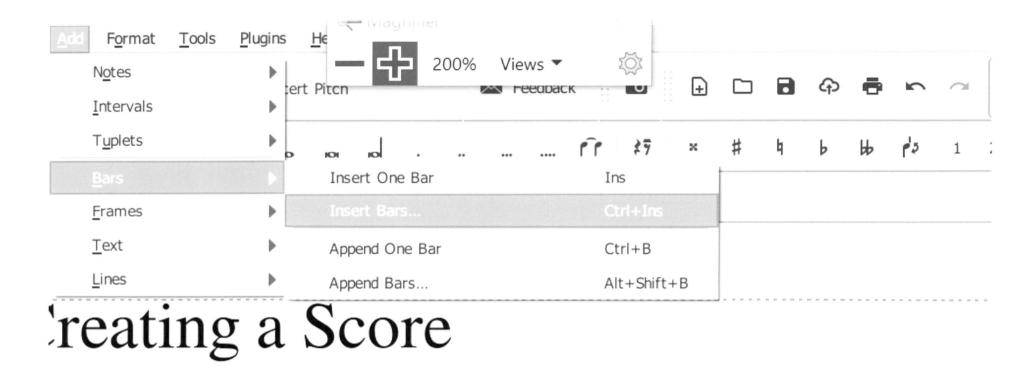

Figure 12.1ee Musescore: adding bars

If you want to change the clef, key or time signature within a piece of music you are working on, highlight where you want the new component to go, then click on View and then Palettes.

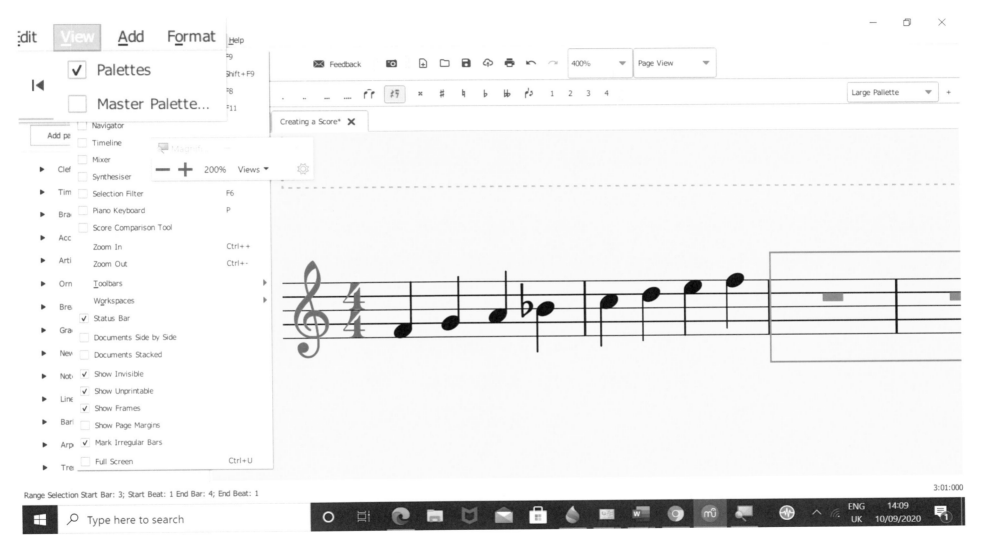

Figure 12.1ff Musescore: changing any component

A list of palettes will appear on the lefthand side. You can only work on one palette at a time. Click on the name of the component you want to change, such as Clefs or Time Signatures.

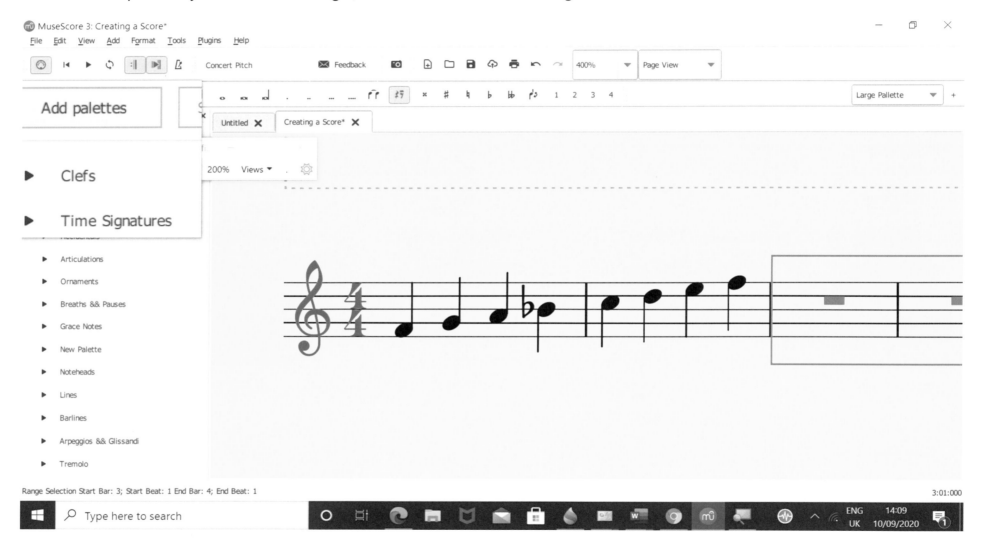

Figure 12.1gg Musescore: choosing a palette

In this picture I have clicked on the Clef palette and chosen a bass clef.

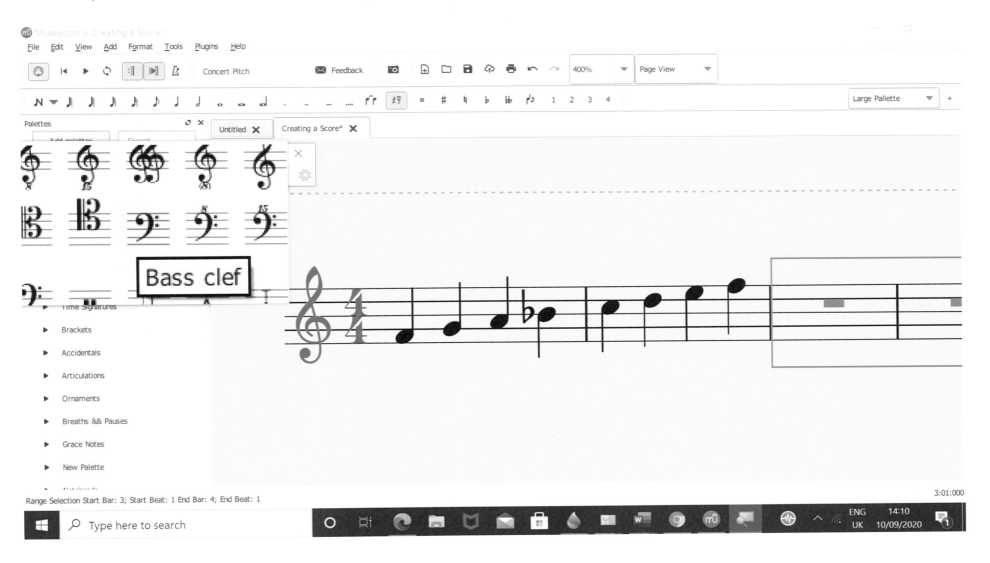

Figure 12.1hh Musescore: choosing a clef

In this picture I have clicked on the Time Signatures palette.

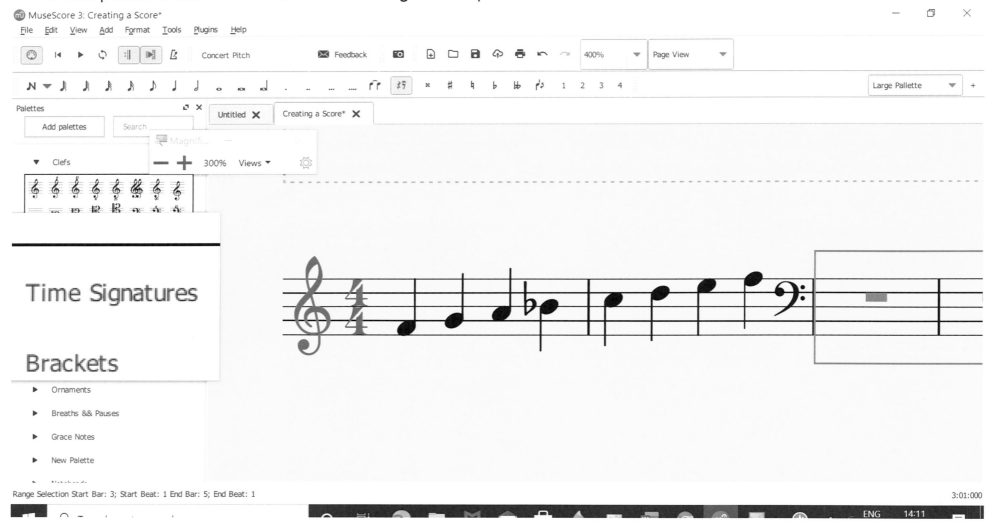

Figure 12.1ii Musescore: finding a time signature

In this picture I have chosen 2/4.

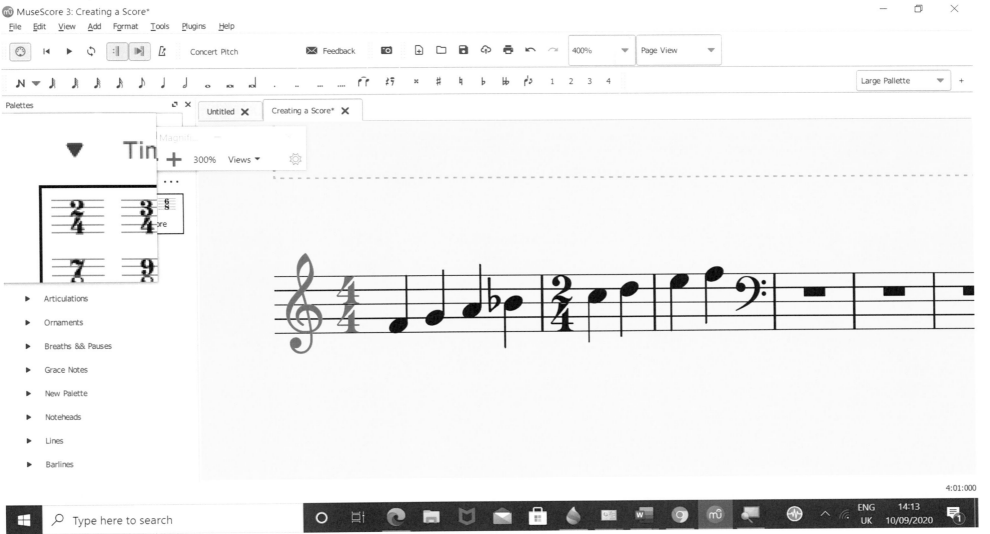

Figure 12.1jj Musescore: choosing a time signature

12. Assistive technology

These are just a few of the things you can do on Musescore but I hope it gives you an idea of how useful it can be when teaching your dyslexic student.

The following are examples of ABRSM mock exams I created on Musescore.

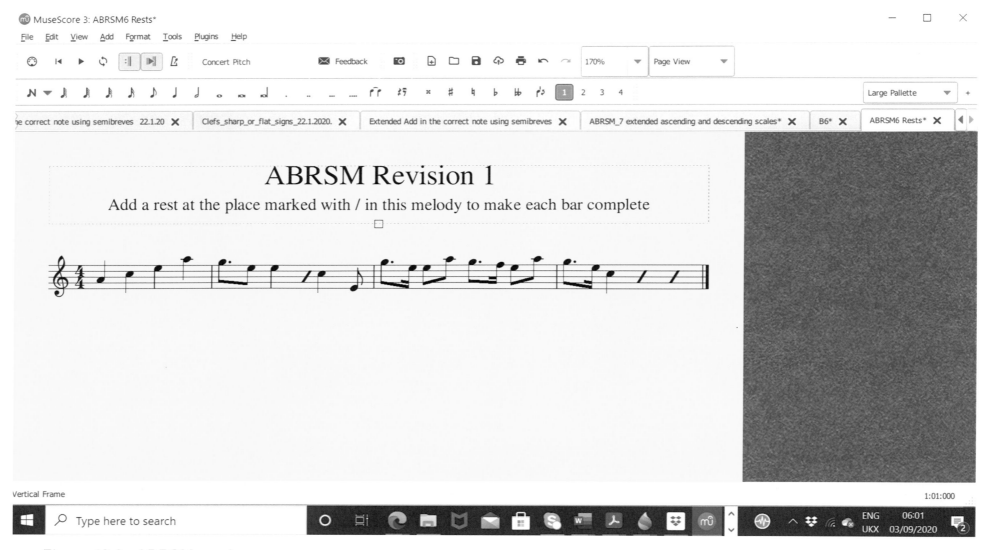

Figure 12.2a ABRSM mock exam

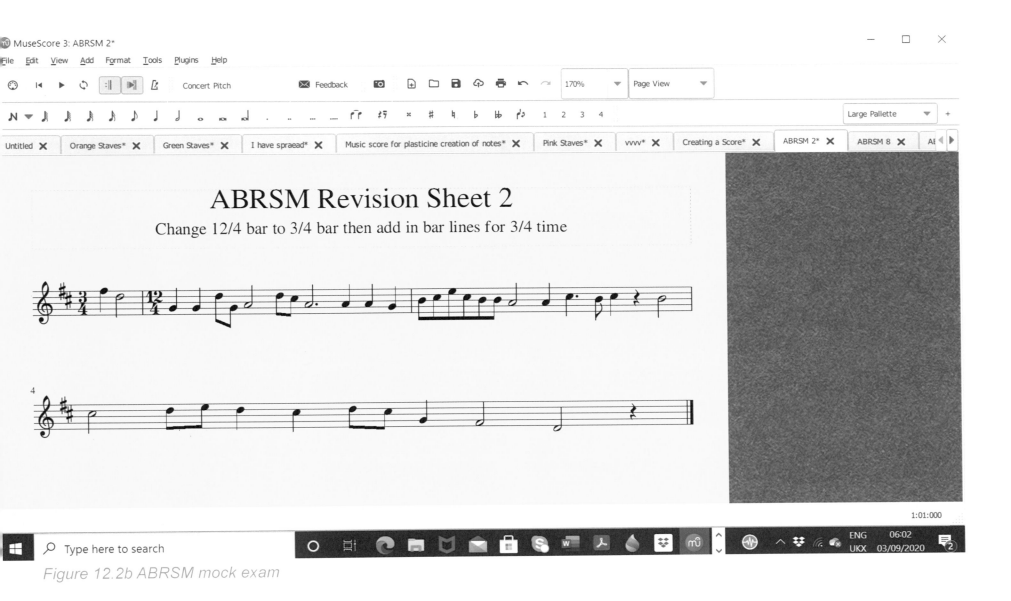

Figure 12.2b ABRSM mock exam

12. Assistive technology

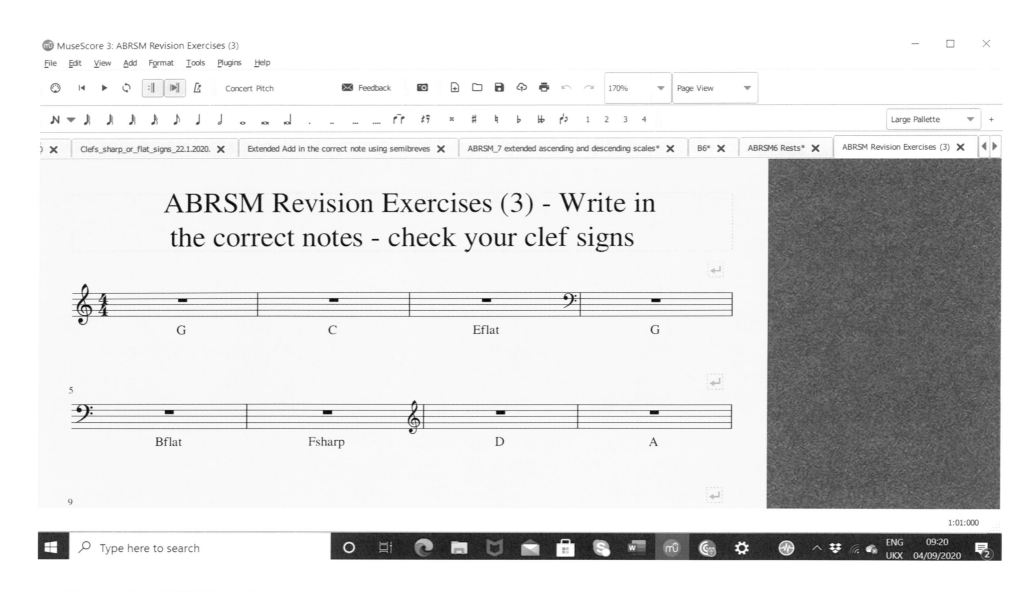

Figure 12.2c ABRSM mock exam

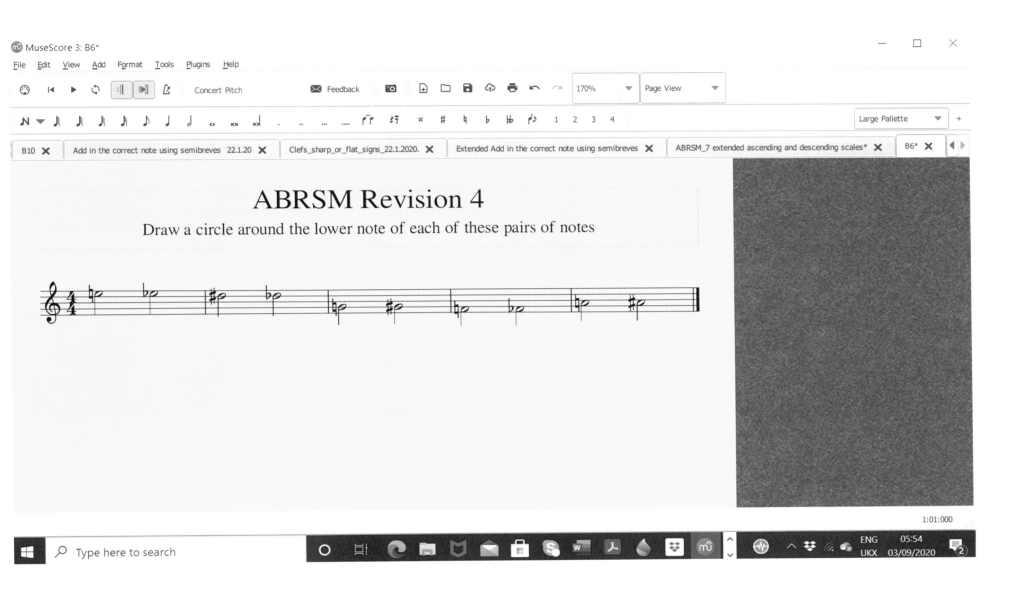

Figure 12.2d ABRSM mock exam

12. Assistive technology

CHECKLIST

After you have opened and explored Musescore:

1. Have you considered training your student using assistive technology?
2. Have you explained to your student that they can display the screen on a television or projector?
3. If your student is not English have you considered providing instructions in their native tongue?
4. Have you created equivalent exam board revision questions so that your student can revise for their exams?

13. CAUSES OF DYSLEXIA

I am the sort of the person who must know WHY. This can be a blessing and a curse, because I rarely accept things at face value. When I began teaching students with dyslexia, I wanted to know what **caused** dyslexia. This final section attempts to distil 40 years of research into a few paragraphs, but I hope that they give you an insight into the causes of dyslexia.

There are many arguments as to the various reasons for dyslexia, but the three most frequently debated are: a deficit in the magnocellular system; a deficit in an individual's phonological processing; and a deficit in the cerebellum in the brain.

MAGNOCELLULAR DEFICIT

There is so much research on this subject that I can only touch on the subject lightly. The magnocellular theory deals predominantly with the problems that a dyslexic has when reading and writing.

A leading world expert, Professor John Stein, and many equally eminent authorities, after many years of research, have stated that dyslexics have problems reading as a result of 'difficulty with auditory and visual sequencing' – auditory sequencing being the ability to produce sounds in a word in the correct order; and visual sequencing being the ability to read words or letters in the correct order (Stein and Walsh, 1997, Vidyasagar and Pammer, 2010).

Sequencing is the process of combining things in a particular order. For a person to be able to read fluently the transient systems in their brain, that is, those responsible for accurately controlling our timing, senses and motor functions, must work correctly. The brain controls every movement our bodies make. We can take no physical or mental action unless our brain has authorised that function. As I am typing this, I am taking it for granted that my fingers will hit the right keys, in the right order, so that I can write this book. And yet, it is far more complicated than that. As I am deciding what to type, my brain is sending a message (an electrical impulse) that travels through my nerves and then connects with the muscles in my palm, forearm and fingers. That electrical signal then commands specific muscles in my hand and fingers to relax, and others to flex or tighten, which allows me to type. Without that message being sent the specific muscles I needed to type this paragraph would not have engaged.

Most people can sequence successfully when reading or listening. However, research tell us that some people have difficulty in forming precise memory images that enable them to sequence sounds and letters, in a word, in the correct order. Successful sequencing depends on accurate timing of auditory and visual sensory inputs from the brain. This is often known as temporal processing.

Transient processing is necessary to control both accurate timing and sensory and motor events, which are vital when playing, practising or composing music. Visual information takes countless twists and turns through the many systems and structures in the brain, before anything can be seen or absorbed.

As you are reading this, your brain is separating where this book is physically in relation to you, and what is in this book. It is also separating out not only each word, but also each letter. It is then spacing them at a sensible distance so that you can read them. Your eyesight is also adapting so that the words are not moving on the page. Your brain is allowing you to engage your auditory senses so that, if you choose to do so, you can sound the words out either aloud or in your mind. At the same time your brain is allowing you to understand the meaning of the words that you are reading. All that in a split second. Isn't that amazing?

As your visual information embarks on its journey along the numerous systems and structures within your brain, it grows in complexity. That visual information eventually splits into two different visual pathways in your brain.

The first pathway is the upper dorsal stream, which helps with spatial understanding, that is, where you are and how you direct your movements in relation to your environment and the items around you. It also helps you to orientate and communicate with the parts of the brain responsible for controlling eye and hand movements.

The second pathway is the lower ventral stream, which helps with identifying, recognising and categorising the things that you see.

Research has shown that these two visual pathways recruit two different kinds of nerve cell to process and carry visual information to other parts of the brain. The first type are the **magnocellular cells**, which help to detect movement and the rate at which something is moving towards you.

The second type are the **parvo cells**, which carry visual information along the ventral stream of the brain and help to sort out visual information about an object's shape, size, colour, clarity, contrast and detail.

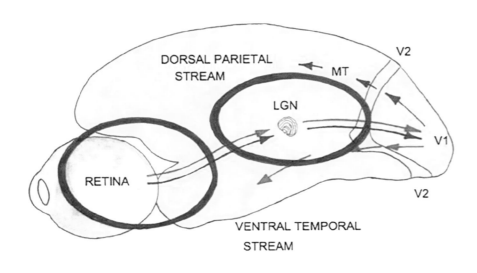

Figure 13.1 Pathways

As you can see, both the magnocellular and parvo cells are vital for correct sequencing and rapid recognition of letters and words.

Reading requires you to rapidly sequence the sounds in words when forming syllables, and phonemes within syllables. This requires the ability not only to accurately hear the changes in the frequency and rise and fall of those sounds, but also to remember their order. Studies have shown that people with developmental dyslexia appear to have less sensitivity to changes in the frequency of the sound being made when trying to correctly pronounce words. This can mean that they are not as precise when sequencing the order of sounds in words (Colling et al., 2017; Kraus et al.,

1996; McAnally and Stein, 1996a; McAnally and Stein, 1996b; Menell et al., 1999).

Studies of brain tissue have found differences in the brains of dyslexic and non-dyslexic persons, particularly in the left hemisphere, which deals with language. Left hemisphere magnocellular layers have been found to be 30% smaller, less organised and significantly thinner (Galaburda et al., 1985; Livingstone et al., 1991; Giraldo-Chica et al., 2015).

The control of eye movements is dependent on magnocellular signals. Studies have shown that dyslexics have less sensitivity to how visual motion impacts on their eye movement. It is important for there to be stable fixation on letters or words for successful reading. That stability is dependent upon the magnocellular system detecting any unwanted eye movements that cause text to move around. This motion signal is sent back to the ocular motor system, which notes the unwanted eye movements, overrides them and directs the eyes back to the words, which then stabilises and fixes the words. If a person has a weaker magnocellular system then they may achieve a less stable visual fixation, which means that the words and letters they are trying to read move around (Singleton and Trotter, 2005; Harries et al., 2015; Singleton and Henderson, 2007).

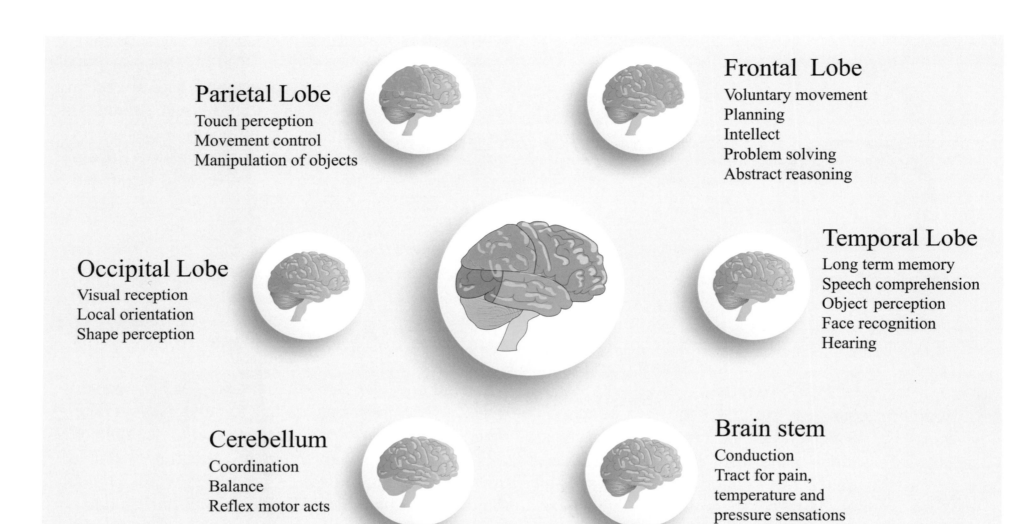

Figure 13.2 Brain functions (source: 123rf.com)

These are just three effects if a person's magnocellular cells are impaired. However, all is not lost as studies have shown that, with certain interventions, there can be an improvement in people with magnocellular difficulties:

1. It has been proven that many dyslexics can gain significant improvements if they read using different coloured overlays (Hall et al., 2014). To date, all of my students have benefited from using coloured overlays, although it should be noted that this doesn't work for everyone.

2. Terri Lawton, a leading expert in this area, has developed a training programme to improve the magnocellular cell responses, which you can find at https://pathtoreading.com/. I always tell my dyslexic students or their parents or guardians about this training programme, so they have the option to investigate it. Please note, I am not a specialist clinician in this area and cannot guarantee the success of this programme.

3. Professor John Stein, who has been studying dyslexia and the magnocellular theory for over 30 years, has found that there are gene variations in dyslexics, and that a lack of omega-3 might be connected to a deficit in the magnocellular cells. Studies are still ongoing and there is no definitive proof at this stage, but a study undertaken by

Professor Stein's colleagues noted that a group of children with poor reading skills and inadequate diets showed an improvement in their reading without any additional support after they were provided with omega-3 supplements. In fact, their reading ability improved by a reading level age of 9 months.

PHONOLOGICAL PROCESSING

Phonological awareness is a broad skill that includes recognising and manipulating units of oral, such as words, syllables, rhymes and onsets (an onset is how a vocal tone is initiated).

Phonological memory is the ability to hold on to speech-based information in your short-term memory, which is necessary when reading text and music. Just imagine reading the word 'phonological', but by the time you have read the 'cal' you have already forgotten the beginning (phono) and the middle (logi). It's not that you don't understand the word, it's just that you can't remember the sound at the beginning of the word. Or imagine reading, 'it was the dead of the night, the moon shimmered in the sky, casting a silver glow over the woods'. Then, when you are asked to repeat the sentence, no matter how hard you try you can only remember that there was a moon and a sky. So you say 'the moon was in the sky'. It would be limiting wouldn't it?

Rapid automatised naming is very important to reading skills as it is the part of phonological processing that allows an automatic, quick and effortless retrieval of the names and sounds of letters, symbols, words, sections of words and rhymes. Remember those times when you have been talking to someone and you can't quite remember a word to describe something, it was exasperating wasn't it?

On a morning walk in the woods with a friend, no matter how hard I tried, I couldn't remember how to say the word 'epidemiologist'. I tried to say it several times, but it just would not come out. I stopped walking and tried to think how to sound the word, it hovered at the back of my brain, but I could not remember the word. Imagine that happening to you every day. And not just once or twice, but numerous times in a day. Can you imagine the frustration you would feel? How it could impact on how you communicate with people?

The question of whether developmental dyslexia is caused by an impairment in phonological processing has been researched for many years. Figure 13.4 shows the different sections of our brain that control different senses and body functions.

The front part of Broca's area is responsible for understanding the meaning of words and is in control of grammatical details and the correct order of words, as required for fluent speech or singing. The back of Broca's area is responsible for helping to understand how words sound.

Broca's area is connected to the Wernicke's area, which is responsible for understanding language and for comprehension, via a group of nerve bundles called the arcuate fasciculus. It is then connected to and bound by the angular gyrus, which is responsible for using sensory information (touch and auditory) to comprehend language.

So you can see that if the Wernicke's area, arcuate fasciculus and angular gyrus are not functioning correctly this will impact on a person's language and memory capabilities. Although a person may not suffer with visual stress, they will still be diagnosed with dyslexia as their ability to read, memorise and recall information is compromised as a result of these differences in the brain.

Figure 13.3 is information gathered from MRI scans to show which sections of the brain are engaged when a dyslexic and a non-dyslexic person are reading. Note that a dyslexic shows increased activity in the Broca's area and less activity in the angular gyrus,

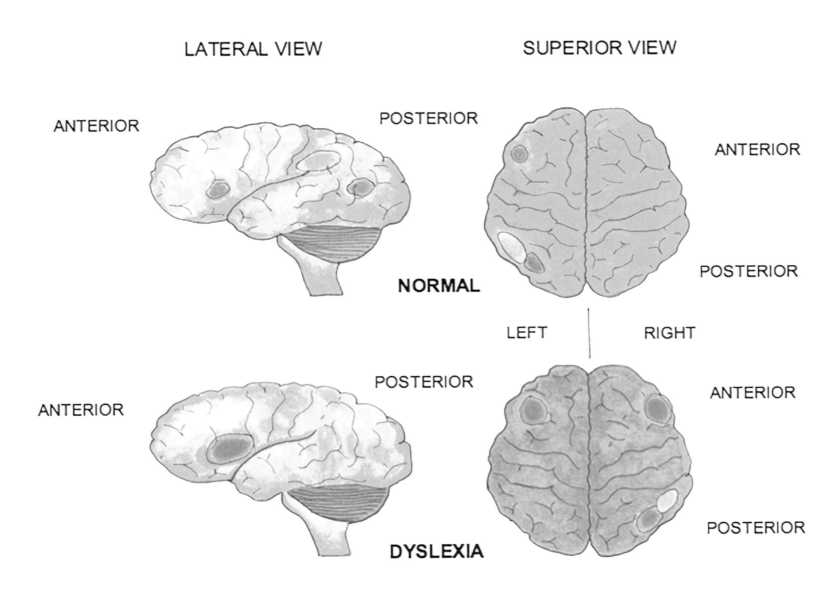

LATERAL VIEW

SUPERIOR VIEW

ANTERIOR

POSTERIOR

ANTERIOR

POSTERIOR

NORMAL

LEFT

RIGHT

POSTERIOR

ANTERIOR

ANTERIOR

POSTERIOR

DYSLEXIA

Figure 13.3 Views of the Broca's area

Wernicke's and arcuate fasciculus sections of the brain, compared with a non-dyslexic.

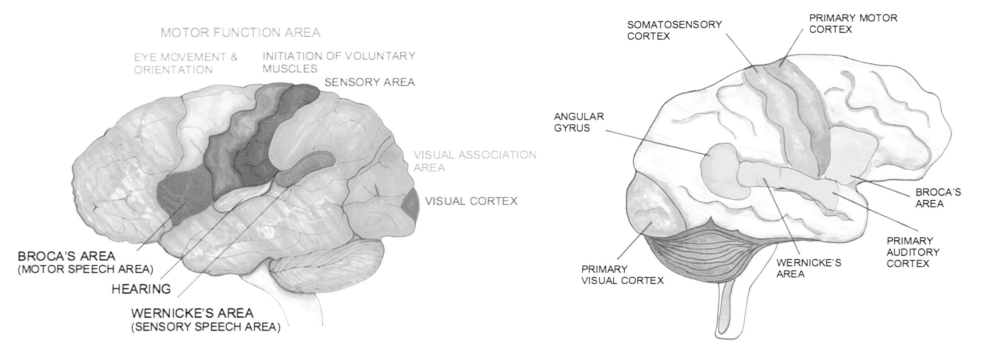

Figure 13.4 Function areas

CEREBELLAR THEORY

The cerebellar theory proposes that the cause of dyslexia is an abnormality in the cerebellum. The cerebellum consists of two hemispheres, connected by the vermis (a narrow midline area), in grey matter and white matter. The grey matter is tightly folded and forms the cerebellar cortex, located on the surface of the cerebellum. It divides into three layers: an external, molecular layer; a middle, Purkinje cell layer; and an internal, granular layer.

The cerebellum is the brain's 'autopilot' for subconsciously and automatically making balanced and skilled movements. It receives a large input from the brain's magnocellular systems for timing and sequencing and it has been shown to be a part of the brain that is one of the most underactive in dyslexics. This leads to, among other things, poor reading and poor physical coordination.

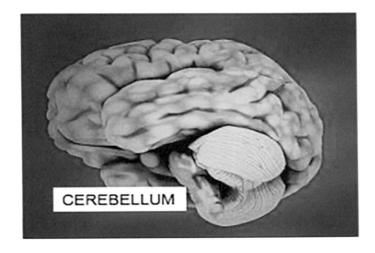

Figure 13.5 Cerebellum (source: Pixabay)

The cerebellum is heavily involved in the eye movements you require for reading and for learning to track a visual target. In 1999, Nicholson et al. measured the degree of activation of the cerebellum in dyslexics and observed that it was significantly lower compared with the activation in normal readers. The cerebellum's function is vital because it has also been established that the right cerebellum, which is connected to the left hemisphere, is very important to speech output and to speech and reading comprehension (Stoodley, 2012). The magnocellular systems also project strongly to the cerebellum, due to the necessity for accurate timing and information for motor control functions.

In 2004, Eckert's research provided proof of structural differences in the cerebellum of dyslexics when compared to non-dyslexics. His research showed that dyslexics displayed less asymmetric cerebella than non-dyslexics who, for the most part, showed a rightward cerebellar asymmetry.

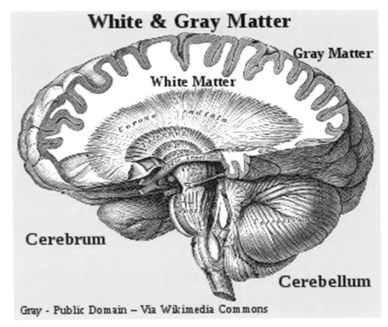

Figure 13.6 White and gray matter (source: Wikimedia Commons)

In 2014, Catherine Stoodley conducted research entitled 'Distinct regions of the cerebellum show grey matter decreases in autism, ADHD, and developmental dyslexia'. Her results showed that in participants with developmental dyslexia, reduced grey matter was located in both the right and left lobules at VI. After this outcome it was suggested that the cerebellar cluster that showed reduced grey matter at VI in the left lobule might contribute to the problems that dyslexics have with visual spatial attention; whereas the cerebellar cluster showing reduced grey matter at V1 in the right lobule might account for difficulties dyslexics have with phonological processing. Especially as the V1 left lobule is engaged in spatial processing and the right lobule is engaged in working memory and language processing.

The above is a very brief overview of the extensive research that has been completed and continues to be undertaken in attempting to establish the cause/s of developmental dyslexia. If you would like to know more about these subjects, please refer to the bibliography at the end of this book.

14. AUDITORY PROCESSING DISORDER

Is your student still struggling? Could they have an auditory processing disorder?

This is another potential cause you may want to consider if your student continues to struggle with intonation and rhythm when learning music. They may have an often overlooked, co-morbid condition that can present with dyslexia – or they may even have been misdiagnosed as having dyslexia and have this condition alone – namely, an auditory processing disorder.

An auditory processing disorder presents itself clinically in the same manner as dyslexia. A review highlighted the difficulties in differentiating between an auditory processing disorder and other developmental language disorders. It concluded that the greatest indicator of an auditory processing disorder, over and above other problems experienced by those with special learning needs, was poorer listening skills. For more details about auditory processing disorders please go to the British Society of Audiology (BSA) website at https://www.thebsa.org.uk/

Auditory processing is the ability to decode, arrange and create auditory information in respect of cognition and behaviour. These are vital skills for "listening comprehension, abstract reasoning and problem solving" that enable a person to understand and adhere to instructions. They are vital when learning music.

A student with an auditory processing disorder has difficulty hearing in a space where there are background sounds, such as:

- the family home
- the classroom
- social situations
- when engaging with other musicians.

The difficulty hearing is due to **an inability to separate the sounds** around them. Therefore auditory processing disorder sufferers tend to mishear words, so they frequently need to ask people to repeat themselves. It can also result in mood swings, tantrums and withdrawal behaviour, due to the sheer frustration of either

1. not being able to hear the instructions they are being given

2. not being able to process the instructions if you give them too quickly.

An auditory processing disorder will manifest itself as:

- poor attention and focus skills
- impairment to speech
- poor auditory memory skills
- greater levels of tiredness as result of the listening demands required of them (BSA, 2018)

The ability to hear clearly is a vital skill for a singer. Unlike speech, where there is one line of sound, a singer, unless singing *a capella*, may have to be aware of a minimum of two layers of sound, namely, the melody vocalised by the singer themselves and a harmonic accompaniment (from a single guitar to a whole orchestra). The greater the level of ensemble work the singer is involved in, the greater the level of focus, auditory discrimination and auditory perception that will be required of them.

CAUSES

The causes of auditory processing disorder are unknown and arguments abound as to whether it is an auditory or a physiological problem.

It is accepted that the hearing mechanism itself may work perfectly, up until the moment the sound arrives in the brain. At this point problems can occur if the brain has difficulty interpreting or recognising the sounds.

At present, there is no specific treatment for an auditory processing disorder. Sound training and adjustments can be put in place to assist the sufferer to cope more effectively with the condition

Recommended adjustments are:

- when communicating aurally with someone with an auditory processing disorder you need to gain their attention prior to engaging them in conversation
- your speech needs to be clear
- you need to emphasise key points
- your sentences should be short
- you should allow time for instructions to be processed
- if you are a fast speaker, you need to slow down.

If you think your student may have an auditory processing disorder (as well as dyslexia or even on its own), then it might be an idea to have a gentle word with the student's parent or guardian.

Why?

Because, although there might already be a diagnosis of dyslexia, the possibility of a misdiagnosis, or a missed diagnosis of auditory processing disorder, might have been overlooked.

There is a substantial body of research on auditory processing issues that goes right back to the late 1940s. So you will understand that I have merely touched on the subject. However, I thought it was important to include it so that you, as a teacher, could consider whether this might be what was impeding your "dyslexic" student's progress.

15. CONCLUSION

Difficulties with dyslexia can result in two courses of action:

- the student gives up music – never an acceptable decision in my world
- or the student fudges it through to their Grade 5 ABRSM Practical exam, passing but rarely getting a merit or distinction, and then continues with music by creating their own group, but not necessarily pursuing the career they might have had as an instrumentalist in the classical field, or as a conductor, or even as a music teacher.

I have seen within my own practice that if dyslexic students are provided with appropriate aids and tools, they can overcome a great many of these difficulties. I cannot begin to describe the excitement and joy I feel when my student and I find the appropriate methods and tools to counteract the difficulties caused by their particular form of dyslexia; nor the wonder in their voice as they can suddenly see the music without it blurring or they begin to beat me in our rhythm games and otherwise develop.

I hope this book helps you find the right set of aids and the best methods to assist your dyslexic students on their musical journeys.

I am sure that when you see the progress they make and watch their confidence grow, it will give you the same joy and pleasure that I gained through teaching my own students.

Wishing you happy teaching.

BIBLIOGRAPHY

Adi-Japha, E., Strulovich-Schwartz, O., & Julius, M. (2011). 'Delayed motor skill acquisition in kindergarten children with language impairment'. Research in Developmental Disabilities, 32, 2963–2971. doi:10.1016/j.ridd.2011.05.005

American Psychiatric Association. (1994). Diagnostic and statistical manual. Washington, DC: Author.

Amitay, S., Ben-Yehudah, G., Banai, K., & Ahissar, M. (2002). Disabled readers suffer from visual and auditory impairments but not from a specific magnocellular deficit. Brain, 125, 2272–2285. doi:10.1093/brain/awf231

Apps, R., and Garwicz, M. (2005). Anatomical and physiological foundations of cerebellar information processing. Nat. Rev. Neurosci. 6, 297–311. doi: 10.1038/nrn1646

Andreou, Eleni; Vlachos, Filippos Learning Styles of Typical Readers and Dyslexic Adolescents Journal of Visual Literacy, 2013, Vol.32(2), p.1. https://gh.abrsm.org/en/making-music/4-the-statistics/

All-Party Parliamentary Group for Dyslexia and other SpLDs, Educational cost of dyslexia - Report October 2019.

Barela J, Dias J L, Godoi, D; Viana A. R, de Freitas; P.B. Postural control and automaticity in dyslexic children: The relationship between visual information and body sway Author links open overlay panel.

Behrmann, Michael M. AT for Students with Mild Disabilities. Intervention in School and Clinic 30.2 (1994): 70-83. Web.

Benmarrakchi, El Kafi, Elhore - Supporting Dyslexic's Learning Style Preferences in Adaptive Virtual Learning Environment dept. of computer science Chouaib Doukkali University, Faculty of Science, El Jadida, Morocco Fz.benmarrakchi@gmail.com, jelkafi@gmail.com,aelhore@gmail.com.

Blackhurst, A.E., 1997. Perspectives on Technology in Special Education. Teaching Exceptional Children, 29(5), pp. 41-48.

Beneventi H, Tønnessen FE, Ersland L. Dyslexic children show short-term memory deficits in phonological storage and serial rehearsal: an fMRI study. Int J Neurosci. 2009;119(11): 2017–2043.

Björklund, M. Dyslexic Students: Success Factors for Support in a Learning Environment. The Journal of Academic Librarianship Volume 37, Issue 5, September 2011, pp. 423–429.

Biotteau M, Chaix Y Albaret, JM. Procedural learning and automatization process in children with developmental coordination disorder and/or developmental dyslexia Human Movement Science Volume 43, October 2015, Pages 78-89.

British Dyslexia Association https://www.bdadyslexia.org.uk/ accessed 23.12.2019, https://www.bdadyslexia.org.uk/advice/children/music-and-dyslexia.

Bonilha, L., Cendes, F., Rorden, C., Eckert, M., Dalgalarrondo, P., Li, L. M., et al. (2008). Gray and white matter imbalance–typical structural abnormality underlying classic autism? Brain Dev. 30, 396–401. doi: 10.1016/j.braindev.2007.11.006

Bradley, L., and Bryant, P. (1983). Categorising sounds and learning to read–a causal connection. Nature 301, 419–421. doi: 10.1038/301419a0

Brambati, S. M., Termine, C., Ruffino, M., Stella, G., Fazio, F., Cappa, S. F., et al. (2004). Regional reductions of gray matter volume in familial dyslexia. Neurology 63, 742–745. doi: 10.1212/01.WNL.0000134673.95020.EE

Brown, W., Eliez, S., Menon, V., Rumsey, J., White, C., and Reiss, A. (2001). Preliminary evidence of widespread morphological variations in the brain in dyslexia. Neurology 56, 781–783. doi: 10.1212/WNL.56.6.781

Brown, R. M., & Robertson, E. M. (2007). Inducing motor skill improvements with a declarative task. Nature Neuroscience, 10, 148–149. doi:10.1038/nn1836

Brown, W. E., Eliez, S., Menon, V., Rumsey, J., White, C., & Reiss, A. (2001). Preliminary evidence of widespread morphological variations of the brain in dyslexia. Neurology, 56, 781–783. doi:10.1212/WNL.56.6.781

Buckner, R. L., Krienen, F. M., Castellanos, A., Diaz, J. C., and Yeo, B. T. (2011). The organization of the human cerebellum estimated by intrinsic functional connectivity. J. Neurophysiol. 106, 2322–2345. doi: 10.1152/jn.00339.2011

Brown, W. E., Eliez, S., Menon, V., Rumsey, J., White, C., & Reiss, A. (2001). Preliminary evidence of widespread morphological variations of the brain in dyslexia. Neurology, 56, 781–783. doi:10.1212/WNL.56.6.781

Cullen, J. et al. (2013) 'The Effects of Computer-Assisted Instruction using Kurzweil 3000 on Sight Word Acquisition for Students with Mild Disabilities', Education & Treatment of Children, 36(2), pp. 87–103. doi: 10.1353/etc.2013.0017.

Diedrichsen, J. (2006). A spatially unbiased atlas template of the human cerebellum. Neuroimage 33, 127–138. doi: 10.1016/j.neuroimage.2006.05.056.

Eckert, M. (2004). Neuroanatomical markers for dyslexia: a review of dyslexia structural imaging studies. Neuroscientist 10, 362–371. doi: 10.1177/1073858404263596.

Doyon, J., & Benali, H. (2005). Reorganization and plasticity in the adult brain during learning of motor skills. Current Opinion in Neurobiology, 15, 161–167. doi:10.1016/j.conb.2005.03.004

Eckert, M. A., Leonard, C. M., Richards, T. L., Aylward, E. H., Thomson, J., & Berninger, V. W. (2003). Anatomical correlates of dyslexia: Frontal and cerebellar findings. Brain: A Journal of Neurology, 126, 482–494. doi:10.1093/brain/awg026

Eckert, M. A., Leonard, C. M., Wilke, M., Eckert, M., Richards, T., Richards, A., et al. (2005). Anatomical signatures of dyslexia in children: unique information from manual and voxel based morphometry brain measures. Cortex 41, 304–315. doi: 10.1016/S0010-9452(08)70268-5

Eickhoff, S. B., Bzdok, D., Laird, A. R., Kurth, F., and Fox, P. T. (2012). Activation likelihood estimation meta-analysis revisited. Neuroimage 59, 2349–2361. doi: 10.1016/j.neuroimage.2011.09.017

Exley, S. (2003). The effectiveness of teaching strategies for students with dyslexia based on their preferred learning styles. British Journal of Special Education, 30, 213-220.

Facoetti, A., Luisa Lorusso, M., Paganoni, P., Umiltà, C., & Gastone Mascetti, G. (2003). The role of visuospatial attention in developmental dyslexia: Evidence from a rehabilitation study. Cognitive Brain Research, 15, 154–164. doi:10.1016/S0926-6410(02)00148-9

Farmer, M. E., & Klein, R. M. (1995). The evidence for a temporal processing deficit linked to dyslexia: A review. Psychonomic Bulletin & Review, 2, 460–493. doi:10.3758/BF03210983

Fawcett, A. J., & Nicolson, R. I. (1995). Persistent deficits in motor skill of children with dyslexia. Journal of Motor Behavior, 27, 235–240. doi:10.1080/00222895.1995.9941713

Fälth, Linda and Svensson, Idor (2015). An app as 'reading glasses' – a study of the interaction between individual and AT for students with a dyslexic profile. (English) In: International Journal of Teaching and Education, ISSN 2336-2022, Vol. 3, no 1, p. 1-12.

Ferretti, G., Mazzotti, S., & Brizzolara, D. (2008). Visual scanning and reading ability in normal and dyslexic children. Behavioural Neurology, 19, 87–92.

Fitts P.M. (1964) - Perceptual-motor skill learning A.W. Melton (Ed.), Categories of human learning, Academic Press, New York (1964), pp. 243-285.

Franceschini, S., Gori, S., Ruffino, M., Pedrolli, K., & Facoetti, A. (2012). A causal link between visual spatial attention and reading acquisition. Current Biology.

Greene, J. C. (2008) 'Is Mixed Methods Social Inquiry a Distinctive Methodology?', Journal of Mixed Methods Research, 2. doi: 10.1177/1558689807309969

Godfriaux Maloy, L. (2014) 'Dyslexia: When keyboard students can't read', Clavier Companion, 6(6), pp. 30–33. Available at: https://search-ebscohost-com.ezproxy.uwtsd.ac.uk/login.aspx?direct=true&db=eue&AN=99204493&site=ehost-live (Accessed: 6 January 2020).

Hatcher J., Snowling, M. and Griffiths, Y. (2002) 'Cognitive assessment of dyslexic students in Higher Education' British Journal of Psychology, Vol 72 No. 1, pp 119-33 https://api.parliament.uk/historic-hansard/commons/1987/jul/13/dyslexia

Harper J A & Ewing N J (1986) A comparison of microcomputer and workbook instructions on reading comprehension of high incidence handicapped children. Educational Technology 26(5) 40-45.

Harris, K. R.., & Graham, S (2013) 'An adjective is a word hanging annals of Dyslexia 63, 65-79. using down from a Noun' Learning to write and students with learning disabilities.

Hauptmann B.R., Reinhart E., Brandt S.A., Karni A (2005): The predictive value of the leveling off of within session performance for procedural memory consolidation - Cognitive Brain Research, 24 (2) pp. 181-189.

Higgins, E. L. and Raskind, M. H. 2000. Speaking to read: The effects of continuous vs. discrete speech recognition systems on the reading and spelling of children with learning disabilities. Journal of Special Education Technology, 15(1): 19–30.

Gabay, Y., Schiff, R. and Vakil, E. (2012) 'Attentional requirements during acquisition and consolidation of a skill in normal readers and developmental dyslexics', Neuropsychology, 26(6), pp. 744–757. doi: 10.1037/a0030235.

Getchell N, Pabreja P, Neeld K, Carrio V. Comparing children with and without dyslexia on the Movement Assessment Battery for Children and the Test of Gross Motor Development. Perceptual and motor skills. 2007; 105(1):207–14. Epub 2007/10/09. https://doi.org/10.2466/pms.105.1.207-214 PMID: 17918566 29.

Goldfarb, L., and Shaul, S. (2013). Abnormal attentional internetwork link in dyslexic readers. Neuropsychology 27, 725–729. doi: 10.1037/a0034422

Hari, R., & Renvall, H. (2001). Impaired processing of rapid stimulus sequences in dyslexia. Trends in Cognitive Sciences, 5, 525–532. doi:10.1016/S1364-6613(00)01801-5

Howard, J. H., Howard, D. V., Japikse, K. C., & Eden, G. F. (2006). Dyslexics are impaired on implicit higher-order sequence learning, but not on implicit spatial context learning. Neuropsychologia, 44, 1131–1144. doi:10.1016/j.neuropsychologia.2005.10.015

Hari, R., & Renvall, H. (2001). Impaired processing of rapid stimulus sequences in dyslexia. Trends in Cognitive Sciences, 5, 525–532. doi:10.1016/S1364-6613(00)01801-5

Hoeft, F., Meyler, A., Hernandez, A., Juel, C., Taylor-Hill, H., Martindale, J. L., et al. (2007). Functional and morphometric brain dissociation between dyslexia and reading ability. Proc. Natl. Acad. Sci. U.S.A. 104, 4234–4239. doi: 10.1073/pnas.0609399104

Howard, J. H., Howard, D. V., Japikse, K. C., & Eden, G. F. (2006). Dyslexics are impaired on implicit higher-order sequence learning, but not on implicit spatial context learning. Neuropsychologia, 44, 1131–1144. doi:10.1016/j.neuropsychologia.2005.10.015

Hynd, G. W., Semrud-Clikeman, M., Lorys, A. R., Novey, E. S., and Eliopulos, D. (1990). Brain morphology in developmental dyslexia and attention deficit disorder/hyperactivity. Arch. Neurol. 47, 919–926. doi: 10.1001/archneur.1990.00530080107018

Iversen S, Berg K, Ellertsen B, Tonnessen FE. Motor coordination difficulties in a municipality group and in a clinical sample of poor readers. Dyslexia (Chichester, England). 2005; 11(3):217–31.

Jednorog, K., Gawron, N., Marchewka, A., Heim, S., and Grabowska, A. (2013). Cognitive subtypes of dyslexia are characterized by distinct patterns of grey matter volume. Brain Struct. Funct. doi: 10.1007/s00429-013-0595-6.

Jueptner, M., & Weiller, C. (1998). A review of differences between basal ganglia and cerebellar control of movements as revealed by functional imaging studies. Brain: A Journal of Neurology, 121, 1437–1449. doi:10.1093/brain/121.8.1437

Keene, S., & Davey, B. (1987) - Effects of computer-presented text on LD adolescents' reading behaviours. Learning Disability Quarterly, 10(4), 283-290.

Kevan, A., & Pammer, K. (2009). Predicting early reading skills from pre-reading measures of dorsal stream functioning. Neuropsychologia, 47, 3174–3181. doi:10.1016/j. neuropsychologia.2009.07.016

Krakauer, J. W., & Shadmehr, R. (2006). Consolidation of motor memory. Trends in Neurosciences, 29, 58–64.

Kibby, M. Y., Pavawalla, S. P., Fancher, J. B., Naillon, A. J., and Hynd, G. W. (2009b). The relationship between cerebral hemisphere volume and receptive language functioning in dyslexia and attention-deficit hyperactivity disorder (ADHD). J. Child Neurol. 24, 438–448. doi: 10.1177/0883073808324772

Krafnick, A. J., Flowers, D. L., Napoliello, E. M., and Eden, G. F. (2011). Gray matter volume changes following reading intervention in dyslexic children. Neuroimage 57, 733–741. doi: 10.1016/j.neuroimage.2010.10.062

Kronbichler, M., Wimmer, H., Staffen, W., Hutzler, F., Mair, A., and Ladurner, G. (2008). Developmental dyslexia: gray matter abnormalities in the occipitotemporal cortex. Hum. Brain Mapp. 29, 613–625. doi: 10.1002/hbm.20425

Luo Y, Wang J, Wu H, Zhu D, Zhang Y. Working-memory training improves developmental dyslexia in Chinese children. Neural regeneration research. 2013.

Moe-Nilssen et al., 2003 R. Moe-Nilssen, J.L. Helbostad, J.B. Talcott, F.E. Toennessen Balance and gait in children with dyslexia Experimental Brain Research, 150 (2003), pp. 237-244

Needle et al., 2006 J.L. Needle, A.J. Fawcett, R.I. NicolsonBalance and dyslexia: An investigation of adults' abilities. European Journal of Cognitive Psychology, 18 (2006), pp. 909-936 Cross Ref View Record in Scopus Google Scholar

Nicholson R.I., Fawcet A.J. (1990) – Automaticity: A new framework for dyslexia research? Cognition 33pp. 159-182.

Nicolson, R., Fawcett, A., and Dean, P. (2001). Developmental dyslexia: the cerebellar deficit hypothesis. Trends Neurosci. 24, 508–511. doi: 10.1016/S0166-2236(00)01896-8

Nicolson, R. I., and Fawcett, A. J. (2007). Procedural learning difficulties: reuniting the developmental disorders? Trends Neurosci. 30, 135–141. doi: 10.1016/j.tins.2007.02.003

Nicolson, R. I., and Fawcett, A. J. (2011). Dyslexia, dysgraphia, procedural learning and the cerebellum. Cortex 47, 117–127. doi: 10.1016/j.cortex.2009.08.016

Pernet, C. R., Poline, J. B., Demonet, J. F., and Rousselet, G. A. (2009). Brain classification reveals the right cerebellum as the best biomarker of dyslexia. BMC Neurosci. 10:67. doi: 10.1186/1471-2202-10-67

Price Geraldine 'Creative solutions to making the technology work Creative solutions to making the technology work: three case studies of dyslexic writers in higher education ALT-J, Research in Learning Technology Vol. 14, No. 1, March 2006, pp. 21–38.

Rae, C., Harasty, J. A., Dzendrowskyj, T. E., Talcott, J. B., Simpson, J. M., Blamire, A. M., et al. (2002). Cerebellar morphology in developmental dyslexia. Neuropsychologia 40, 1285–1292. doi: 10.1016/S0028-3932(01)00216-0

Ramus F, Pidgeon E, Frith U. The relationship between motor control and phonology in dyslexic children. Journal of child psychology and psychiatry, and allied disciplines. 2003; 44(5):712–22. Epub 2003/07/02. PMID: 12831115 26.

Redford, K. kredford@mcds. or. (2019) 'Assistive Technology: Promises Fulfilled: From a teacher's perspective, assistive technology delivers on its potential to transform learning experiences for students with—and without—learning disabilities', Educational Leadership, 76(5), pp. 70–74. Available at: https://search-ebscohost-com.ezproxy.uwtsd.ac.uk/login.aspx?direct=true&db=eue&AN=134555685&site=ehost-live (Accessed: 13 March 2020).

Richlan, F. (2012). Developmental dyslexia: dysfunction of a left hemisphere reading network. Front. Hum. Neurosci. 6:120. doi: 10.3389/fnhum.2012.00120

Richlan, F., Kronbichler, M., and Wimmer, H. (2009). Functional abnormalities in the dyslexic brain: a quantitative meta-analysis of neuroimaging studies. Hum. Brain Mapp. 30, 3299–3308. doi: 10.1002/hbm.20752

Rochelle KS, Talcott JB. Impaired balance in developmental dyslexia? A meta-analysis of the contending evidence. Journal of child psychology and psychiatry, and allied disciplines. 2006; 47 (11):1159–66. Epub 2006/11/02. https://doi.org/10.1111/j.1469-7610.2006.01641.x PMID: 17076755 28

Saine Lerkkanen Marja-Kristiina, Ahonen, Tolvanen Lyytinen - Predicting word-level reading fluency outcomes in three contrastive groups: Remedial and computer-assisted remedial reading intervention, and mainstream instruction - Learning and Individual Differences Volume 20, Issue 5, October 2010, Pages 402-414.

Senatore et al., Rhythmic gymnastics and dyslexia: a two-year preliminary case study Journal of Physical Education and Sport, suppl. Supplement issue 5; Pitesti (Nov 2018)

Siok, W. T., Niu, Z., Jin, Z., Perfetti, C. A., and Tan, L. H. (2008). A structural-functional basis for dyslexia in the cortex of Chinese readers. Proc. Natl. Acad. Sci. U.S.A. 105, 5561–5566. doi: 10.1073/pnas.0801750105

Snowling, M (1987) Dyslexia: A cognitive Developmental Practice, Basil Blackwell, Oxford.

Stampoltzis, A., Antonopoulou, E., Zenakou, E. & Kouvava, S. (2010). Learning sensory modalities and educational characteristics of Greek dyslexic and non-dyslexic university students. Electronic Journal of Research in Educational Psychology, 8, 561-580.

Stoodley, C. J., and Schmahmann, J. D. (2010). Evidence for topographic organization in the cerebellum of motor control versus cognitive and affective processing. Cortex 46, 831–844. doi: 10.1016/j.cortex.2009.11.008

Stoodley, C. J., and Stein, J. F. (2011). The cerebellum and dyslexia. Cortex 47, 101–116. doi: 10.1016/j.cortex.2009.10.005

Stoodley, C. J., and Stein, J. F. (2013). Cerebellar function in developmental dyslexia. Cerebellum 12, 267–276. doi: 10.1007/s12311-012-0407-1

Stoodley C. J., Distinct regions of the cerebellum show gray matter decreases in autism, ADHD, and developmental dyslexia Department of Psychology, American University, Washington, DC, USA, Front. Syst. Neurosci., 20 May 2014 | https://doi.org/10.3389/fnsys.2014.00092

Verly, M., Verhoeven, J., Zink, I., Mantini, D., Peeters, R., Deprez, S., et al. (2014). Altered functional connectivity of the language network in ASD: role of classical language areas and cerebellum. Neuroimage Clin. 4, 374–382. doi: 10.1016/j.nicl.2014.01.008

Yang, J., Peng, J., Zhang, D., Zheng, L. And Mo, L., 2017. Specific effects of working memory training on the reading skills of Chinese children with developmental dyslexia. PLoS One, 12(11).

Lightning Source UK Ltd
Milton Keynes UK
UKRC030411090223
416683UK00001B/4